FREE 💡 THE
GENIUS

How the Very Best Grow Their
Meaning, Mission, and Contribution

DAVID MARTIN

ISBN-13: 978-1793062222

For bulk purchase and for booking, contact:

David Martin

letsconnect@davidmartinco.com

(513) 533-9339

www.DavidMartinCo.com

Full Reviews for FREE THE GENIUS

"David Martin showed me how to 'free my genius' and build a seven-figure speaker/trainer business. I'd follow him to hell and back... as long as I could take this book with me."

—Scott Mann, Former Green Beret and Best-Selling Author of *Game Changers*

"David Martin is the most caring and capable counsel I've ever had. His ability to see through walls, around corners, and into the hearts and minds of individuals, teams, and communities is superhuman. Let him help you free your genius like he has for me."

—Mike Wisler, CIO of M&T Bank

"David possesses a rare gift: The ability to translate powerful insights clearly and simply to inspire meaningful action. David's wisdom has made more impact on my professional development and in my career advancement than anyone or anything, including an Ivy League degree. From my own experience, I recommend David as one of the few people who knows how to help you make significant progress toward your most inspired goals and toward becoming the person who is eagerly awaiting to burst forward and make a powerful impact in your world."

—Ryan Halverson, Sr. HR Leader, McKesson Corp

"For nearly 20 years, David has been a coach and mentor to me, a deep and constant source of insights and wisdom. As you'll find in *Free the Genius*, he's a great storyteller. He succinctly synthesizes timeless observations of the human condition into practical and actionable advice. He has a gift for re-framing a standard problem or dilemma such that you'll discover many new paths to move forward."

—Ray Peloso, CEO of Katabat

"David is an amazing coach and mentor, equipping you with the tools and habits you need to develop in a sustainable way as both a leader and a human being. His ability get deep and help focus on the areas with the highest leverage is outstanding. Along my journey, he provided both the direct feedback needed along with caring support."

—Devin Lipawsky, VP HR, Capital One

"This book is a gem. David Martin's work is truly powerful, at times profound, and always positively impactful. His commitment to seeing the light in each of us is unflinching. He's unlike any other coach. His sense of humor and fantastic storytelling skills make his work particularly sticky. He can 'Free the Genius' in you."

—Anne Chambers, Founder Certifiably/Red212

"For over a decade, David has been my secret weapon as I've navigated many companies, industries, and teams. Along the way, his insights and teaching have driven me to self-discovery, pushing me to reach my dreams on my terms and be the best version of myself. His coaching has transformed my teams… unleashing our individual and collective power, changing our lives and the lives of our customers along the way. I'm thrilled that he's taken the time to write down his insights, and I know you'll learn a tremendous amount from his unique storytelling ability and encouraging spirit."

—Keri Gohman, Chief Platform Business Officer, President of Xero Americas, Xero

"Anyone who wants to elevate their game owes it to themselves to incorporate these ideas into their daily practice. David has an uncanny ability to identify the behaviors, motivations, and experiences that contribute to your strengths and challenges as a leader, and he has translated complex research into practical frameworks to guide better and more effective decisions. David's guidance has dramatically accelerated my development as a leader and improved my understanding of how to do my job more effectively."

—Bob Youakim, CEO of Passport Labs

"David is masterful in distilling complex information down into easy to understand and appreciate little gems of wisdom—just like he's done in *Free the Genius*. He'll guide you to a deeper understanding of what most important to you. He's whip smart, deeply caring, and likes to have fun while leading the way on the path of transformation and personal empowerment. From a more personal perspective, David helped me move from a place of feeling overwhelmed by the many roles I need to play each day to finding and focusing on the glue in the middle that holds my life together. Focusing on what matters most, I feel more empowered and happy at home, at work, and in all the (many) places in between."

—Kate Noble, entrepreneur, mother, teacher/coach, owner/
director of Shine Yoga & Integrated Wellness

"David has a very rare, precious and uncanny ability to deeply understand a person—pinpoint individual strengths, diagnose weaknesses, isolate leadership Kryptonite—and provide extremely personalized, customized counsel that unleashes otherwise-pent-up leadership potential. The impact he has on his clients extends well beyond the workplace. He is truly gifted and any counsel from him—whether 15 minutes over coffee or a book full of wisdom—is a priceless gift."

—Jessica George, Agency Strategy, Empower

"David combines great common sense with wonder and unwavering confidence that we all have gifts to give; his optimism and sense of joy are infectious and have helped me to grow both personally and professionally."

—Mona Jantzi, Chief Experience Officer of Barclaycard

"When you're the leader whose work is to inspire and challenge others, who does this for YOU when you've hit a plateau? This is the where David Martin shines. His broad experience has given him a unique and valuable insight into helping LEADERS grow. You've helped others, now it's time to allow David to help you."

—Reuben Carranza, Global President of Beauty Industry Company

"An essential read for anyone looking to find and cultivate their own personal genius. In an age of endless content and media overload, David's bite-sized insights are a welcome resource for everyone from time-starved senior executives to anyone simply looking for some quick inspiration and motivation. He expertly packages his nuggets of wisdom in easily digestible stories that are readily applied and a joy to consume."

—Zach Rieken, CEO, Living Proof

"David Martin possesses a truly rare ability to cut through the noise of what is getting in your way, then constructively and compassionately guiding you to discover your talents and values, unleashing the leadership potential (your genius) that is often so tough to see on your own. I'm a better human and a better leader because of our nearly a decade of work together."

—Jeff Elgin, Chief Technology Officer of Home Care Delivered

"So many self-development courses and books are based in the success principles—think positively, be better, focus on success and the money will follow, etc. Sometimes motivation isn't enough to be positive. I engaged with those theories, but it wasn't enough to drown out a destructive inner voice. I was ready as a student and ready for the teacher. David went deeper into what to actually do, the lasting practical steps on taking control of my subconscious, identifying the conversation with myself and quickly being able to turn my perspective around and in turn, my life."

—Iain Jones, Creative, Barefoot Proximity

"David Martin helped me build a foundation that has served me well for over 15 years. It's allowed me to 'free the genius' and grow my leadership through multiple steps of my career, from operational leader to the executive level."

—Beth Himes, Vice President of Commercial Service Operations, Aetna

"Here's what learning from David will do for you. David puts himself in the middle of a story. As he shares a personal experience, I see my team gaining interest. Trust is earned. Laptops close. The team is more interactive than I could have imagined. I wonder… 'how could I do this with a group of strangers?' Now, let him guide you."

—Rob Lupini, Director of Sales, GERDAU Special Steel North America

ACKNOWLEDGEMENTS

I am grateful for the amazing support of so many people who helped create this book.

Thank you, first, to my most important editor, friend, teacher, and love of my life, Brenda. This book and the Genius Farm wouldn't exist without you. You are an angel on earth. You make this extremely fun.

Thank you to Deb Buxton, my work ally and steadfast friend of 15 years who has remained the foundation of this team. Everything you touch is better.

Scott Mann, my friend, colleague, teacher, and brother. Thank you for kicking my ass… errr… I mean for encouraging me to write this book. Kathy Quinn, the strategy ninja. You're such an amazing mash-up of brilliance and heart, and your laughter and wisdom is a bright light for the world. For my fellow Mastermind members who hold the bar high and inspire me, Jerry Lujan, Greg Parsons, and Scott Mann.

Thank you to my two young and dedicated teachers, José Cabrera and Egyptian Banks, my Brothers. Your dedication to keep freeing your genius inspires me to never stop making my work more accessible to all people. You teach us that it's not just where you come from but where you're going and that anything is possible through dedicated work.

Thank you to Linda, Carol, and Donna Martin, sisters, friends, teachers, and instigators. "EvandDick's" legacy is ours to carry now. And to Grandpa Nye, the instigator of all of this.

Thank you to my many, many teachers who have inspired and reshaped me and my work over decades: Brenda Villa, Chuck Olson,

Bonnie Bachman, Julio Olalla, Sally Kempton, Sianna Sherman, Mitchel Bleier, Kate Noble, Gino Fontana, Kurt Kleman, Kathy Quinn, Ed Byrd, George Leonard, Edmond Antoine, Maricarmen Guell, Josephina Santiago, Terrie Lupberger, Scott Coady, Gary Mitchiner, Babette Bourgeois, Bo Eason, Tim Adams, Mary Kincaid, Karen Mozes, Toby Christensen, Alan Weiss, Kathy McDonald, and David Muth.

I'm grateful for these accomplished people, even those I've never met, whose example of living inspired one or more chapters: José Cabrera, Scott Mann, Cooper Mann, Rex Mann, Sarah Reckmeyer, Jeff Stipp, Sally Kempton, Nye Martin, Dick Martin, Naod Haile, Lakpa Gelu, Ron Chernow, Daniel Coyle, Kate Flannery, Madonna, Bruce Springsteen, Sylvester Stallone, Matt Damon, the Chicago Cubs, Willson Contreras, Theo Epstein, Anson Dorrance, Kobe Bryant, Lin-Manuel Miranda, Elon Musk, Warren Buffett, Abraham Lincoln, Angelique Kerber, Serena Williams, Morgan William, Gwen Jorgensen.

Thank you to the most amazing clients who keep challenging me and teaching me. There are far too many to name, but special thanks to those who challenged our team to design something new that now lives in this book: Ray Peloso, Amanda Aghdami, Heather Cox, Mike Wisler, Don Busick, Keri Gohman, John Polk, Ryan Halverson, Anne Chambers, Jeff Holland, Wendy Forster, John Christman, Martha Eskew, Jerry Welch, Mike Flannery, Mike Caslin, Erik Birkerts, Liz Ruby, Cheryl Walker Shapero, and Melonie Garrett.

Thank you to my clients who generously shared your reviews of my work and of this book. I admire how you are changing the world.

Thank you Danaan Perry for your beautiful writing at the end of Chapter 22 that has inspired so many people, especially me, since the first time I read it.

Thank you to the awesome team at Ignite Press, real pros and genuinely good people who made publishing a book far easier than I expected it to be—Everett O'Keefe, Malia Sexton, and Samantha Maxwell. Immense thanks to my personal editors, writing and recording coaches Shannon Bromenschenkel, Carrie Herzner, and Cary Maish Brodie.

I'm fortunate to have the support of so many—all of you, Geniuses.

Dedication

*To Dad and Mom, "DickandEv." I studied with teachers around the
world to learn that you'd taught me all I needed.*

*And to Brenda. Your inspiration and voice is in
every page of this book.*

TABLE OF CONTENTS

FOREWORD

There's a genius in all of us.

This is the lifelong mantra of my great friend David Martin and the basis for his wonderful new book, *Free the Genius: How the Very Best Grow Their Meaning, Mission, and Contribution.* A collection of inspiring short stories pulled from David's personal life and his work with others, this book celebrates the exceptionalism of ordinary people. David has dedicated his life to helping people realize their own unique genius so they can make a difference in the world in the way they've always dreamed of.

Throughout his career, David has found again and again that the people drawn to him are the ones who are called to do big things. They are compelled to make a meaningful contribution. In David, they find an ally who understands all too well the intense series of challenges they have overcome or are struggling to at this very moment. It's important to dream big, but when failure happens—and it almost always does—it can be what holds you back.

As these challenges present themselves, David and this book will be here for you when it matters most, helping you reframe failure, master the process of change (not just fall in love with its outcome), and build an unbreakable resiliency. You will see these stories of inspiration throughout the book, such as a basketball player who overcame all odds against him to excel on the court or an undocumented immigrant who could not read at 12 years old but now works in Washington, D.C., lobbying for immigration reform for other young people in need. And you will find the one story that exactly mirrors what you are experiencing or feeling at any given moment.

David's stories have an underlying sweetness and innocence. They celebrate the everyday. They are relatable. And because they are, they help you reflect and apply the story and insight to the life you have right now versus something "out there" that often feels unattainable.

David has been a close friend and colleague for 10 years. His superpower is his ability to help you "hear" in a way where you do not feel threatened or ashamed all while helping you navigate your way through a volley of emotions and setbacks.

This book serves as a reminder of your own genius qualities. It may even help you discover those powerful qualities for the first time.

I can tell you that this book is not mere advice but the genuine message of a person who "walks the walk and talks the talk." A person who blends humility and humor. I have never met anyone who believes in and champions the underdog more.

You are about to take an incredibly fulfilling journey to realize your true potential, what David calls, "living life fully expressed." With David's help, I can't wait for you to Free the Genius.

—Kathy Quinn, The Q Group, LLC, Chicago

HOW GENIUS GETS LOST (AND FOUND) IN A BUSY WORLD

My phone rang at 7:30 on a Monday morning. It was my client Frank. Though we didn't have a call scheduled, he sometimes used his long morning commute to call me for real-time guidance. Anticipating his usual enthusiasm, I answered the phone.

A very different version of Frank was on the phone that morning, though. Frank was a smart and talented person: President of a global business based in New York. He was a rock-star leader on a mission. But that morning, he let me know he was not at his best.

"Good morning, Frank. How are you?"

"I'm not good."

"Oh, I'm sorry to hear that. What's up?"

"I think I could lose my job today."

"Wow! Ok, you definitely have my attention. Tell me what's going on."

"Well, when I went to bed last night, this wasn't on my calendar. But when I got up this morning, I have a new appointment… at 11 a.m. with the CEO and a member of the Board… at their request. That can't be good." He sighed. "You know they fire people on Mondays…"

Anyone but Frank would've known in that moment that he was probably being a bit delusional. But to Frank, the "head trash" he was listening to was very real and very ominous. Perhaps you're familiar with "head trash": the self-critical doomsday voice in your head that can take over and manipulate your mindset.

Frank is a genius. You might be thinking he doesn't sound like such a genius. What genius believes he's going to lose his job because of a new appointment on his calendar? But Frank was dealing with an enormous challenge at work. And often, the high stress of challenges makes our head trash grow louder.

Bottom line, Frank was far more brilliant than he thought he was in that moment. He'd just lost track of it. For many people I've worked with, "head trash" isn't just a Monday-morning thing. It's a 24/7 thing.

It's my job, and mission, to help people like Frank—bright, inspired leaders, performers, coaches, teachers, moms, dads—access their genius.

Within a few minutes, Frank was back in a better frame of mind and off the phone with me. It didn't take long for him to discover he'd made the whole problem up in his head. I asked him to call me after his meeting with the CEO to let me know what happened.

It turned out to be a pretty humorous misunderstanding after the fact. The CEO had scheduled the meeting to ask Frank for advice, not to fire him. Listen to Frank's full story here: www.davidmartinco.com/ftg-videos.

In spite of how it might seem, **there is nothing wrong with Frank**. In fact, Frank is normal. Extremely normal. Deep down, he's a person on a mission to do good work in the world—to create big change that will change people's lives for the better. Work was his platform, his way to make his contribution to society.

Does any of this sound familiar?

If you picked up this book called *Free the Genius*, I'd guess you're aware of your potential, but you're not always sure how to cultivate or express it. You care deeply about the work you do and the people you serve, and you want to express your best self in all that you do. Yet, you know that doing good work is rarely easy, even when your intentions are positive. Often, we're the greatest obstacles on our paths.

I wrote this book for Frank. I wrote this book for you.

I work with people who want to do big work that matters to them. Regardless of their roles in life, they're each on a mission to change their part of the world for the better.

Does that describe you? **If so, you probably recognize at some level that your mission will require more of you—more than is comfortable, more than you've ever brought forth before, maybe more than you realize you're capable of. I call that being fully expressed.**

Surprisingly, bringing all of yourself full-on without holding back is one of the most difficult and seemingly risky things any of us can do. But it's also the most natural and the most rewarding journey: to Free Your Genius.

The challenge is that perceived risk that haunts most people: What if I stick my neck out that far and fail? Or what if I go for it and get rejected? That potential risk is enough to cause most people to just leave the Genius in the bottle.

To live and lead at that level, you need to Free the Genius.

What is Genius, and how can you free it?

There are some very limiting definitions of "genius" floating around, today. Genius is not simply determined by your IQ, job title, or the ability to do math in your head.

Even if you and I have never met, I know a few things about you. Although every person is unique, there are human themes and patterns that are universal across time, geography, and cultures. I have advised and consulted, coached, trained, and guided thousands of bright people across the globe for more than two decades. **I promise you that any struggle you have to free your genius is not a personal shortcoming. It's a universal human challenge.**

You came fully loaded with all you need. Your challenge is to free the genius and bring it to life. Because I've walked this path with so many people already, I know with absolute confidence that owning even a fraction more of your unclaimed wisdom and talent will be profound for you.

I'm not suggesting that doing this will be easy. **Many of the ideas in this book run counter to modern day "common sense"—theories that most people have come to accept over the last century yet hold us back.**

This book is full of stories of real people who've stopped unconsciously overlooking or squelching their genius within. As you read their stories, you'll connect with their challenges and their ideas for how to navigate them skillfully. **For example, take my client Liz.**

Liz is ridiculously talented. She's as much a magician as a business leader. She consistently pulls rabbits out of hats to the amazement of anyone watching. One of her specialties is taking a business that seems hopelessly off the rails and systematically turning the people and the business around at rapid speed.

She's done this at several companies. She's respected and valued for her ability to accomplish things that others say can't be done.

Once, after sharing with her some very positive feedback I'd heard about her ability to see a clear solution in the chaos, she looked at me perplexed and asked, "Doesn't everyone do that?" She wasn't aware of how brilliant she was. She thought it was a universal talent.

Liz is a genius. Everyone else could see it. She was the only one who didn't. Not surprisingly, as she started to appreciate some of her exceptional qualities, aka superpowers, she began to leverage them more consistently. Her meaning, mission, and contribution grew.

She was freeing her genius.

Perhaps you're like Liz. Everyone else can see your superpowers, but you're blind to the best in yourself.

When overcoming a difficult challenge, you too may ask, "Can't everyone do that?"

Definitely not.

Now, consider my client Jorge. Jorge was facing the biggest challenge of his career: the multi-billion, 10,000-person business he'd led for two years was doing quite well. Where's the challenge in that, right? But Jorge could see beyond the current success. He saw an opportunity that no one else, including the CEO, believed was possible.

It's one thing to get people to rally around solving a problem when they're feeling the pain of it. It's another situation entirely to enroll people in a better approach when they like the current one just fine. Success can be a great sedative. It puts people to sleep, keeping them from seeing opportunities to keep improving.

But Jorge's genius was wide awake. And because he listened to his genius despite no one else being able to see what he was seeing, he boldly declared to senior leadership he was going to change things radically for the better.

There was one small problem... he didn't quite know how!

Over the course of 24 months, he struggled to lead the change. First, the internal headwinds of resistance were strong. Also, most of the territory he and his teams encountered was uncharted. It was an epic challenge that could be its own case study. Ultimately, Jorge and his team inspired the creation of a new business model for the entire company. Even the CEO acknowledged later that they'd accomplished something he once believed was not only unnecessary but impossible. **The intense pressure of the impossible challenge inspired the untapped genius in Jorge, his team, and eventually all of them to emerge.**

The seed of their genius always existed, but it needed to be cultivated to grow. Jorge and his genius led the way.

Sometimes you're like Frank, and you tell yourself stories that squelch your genius.

Sometimes you're like Liz, unaware of your superpowers and not fully expressing the very best of yourself.

Sometimes you're like Jorge, and you don't realize what brilliance lies dormant within you until you face an extreme challenge.

This book is for the versions of Frank, Liz, and Jorge that live in you.

I'm committed to helping you release your great brilliance into the world.

Let's get started.

HOW TO USE THIS BOOK

You can drop in to this book at any place and at any time and take away insights. Each chapter stands alone—you need not read it from cover to cover. Open it when you need it. The fundamentals are shared mostly in short stories to spark your own insight so that a busy person like you can apply them quickly. To make it easy to navigate, I've grouped the chapters by six key sections—six themes that commonly arise when I'm working with people.

This isn't a how-to book or a book of answers. I've found that my clients don't need answers. They want to be challenged to think in a new way. I teach them how. From there, they find their own answers. In *Free the Genius*, you'll find your own answers too.

The phenomenon of untapped genius is so universal among people that, even though we may have never met, I feel like I know you already. And we're going to do great work together. So let's begin…

Let's **Free the Genius.**

P.S. I have a personal favor to ask. A book's impact is often determined by the reviews it receives. If you feel so inclined after becoming familiar with this book, I would deeply appreciate your online review. You can leave a review wherever the book was the purchased.

WELCOME TO THE GENIUS FARM

Every month, different clients travel to the Genius Farm,* our HQ, a place where we cultivate the light of their genius. People from all walks of life: individuals, teams, and ad hoc groups facing an extreme challenge/opportunity. In the intensive sessions we create, they move through a process to help them rapidly free their genius to make big leaps in their performance and their contribution. We call it work, but Genius Farm "work" is full of energy and laughter. Genius is easier to access when you're having fun.

People leave more clear, more confident, and with a plan to act boldly to create great impact.

Have you ever noticed how a sports stadium feels grandiose and ready for greatness, a music hall feels reverent and ready to invite artistry, and a campground feels grounded and quiet even when the space isn't in use? Locations carry their own "vibe" simply because they've been used in a specific way so many times. The feeling is palpable and contagious. In a similar way, the Genius Farm has developed its own vibe. Visitors have said they feel more clarity, creativity, and boldness when they're here.

---

* Why do we call it the Genius Farm?
   I'm a fourth-generation farmer. My dad, grandpa, and great-grandpa cultivated life that was ultimately harvested as grain. I help you cultivate life, the light of your genius, that you'll cultivate as results—growing your meaning, mission, and contribution to the world.

The vibe of the Genius Farm birthed this book. I hope you'll feel some of that for yourself as you read… Of course, it's already in you, and this book will help you reconnect with it.

I'm a fourth-generation farmer. My dad, grandpa, and great-grandpa cultivated life that was ultimately harvested as grain. I help you cultivate life, the light of your genius, that you'll cultivate as results—growing your meaning, mission, and contribution to the world.

⦿ SECTION I:

YOUR GENIUS FOUNDATION:
THE MASTERY MINDSET

Freeing the Genius isn't always easy, but it's also not a mystery. Your constant companion in setting free the best of yourself is your Mastery Mindset, and the stories in this section strengthen your connection to that part of yourself.

The Mastery Mindset is a choice to take a dedicated, consistent approach to being your best—fully authentic and fully expressed. The reward is that you keep feeling more alive and strong year after year.

The Mastery Mindset isn't a flash of inspiration that flames and fades. It becomes the momentum that carries you through your most difficult moments.

The biggest reason most people leave talent on the table is because they expect their best to just appear when they need it, instead of cultivating it steadily when the pressure and the stakes are low. They give their attention to the urgencies of the moment, running from crisis to crisis instead of choosing to invest strategically and steadily in learning—which will pay off exponentially over time.

 go to www.davidmartinco.com/ftg-videos

Freeing the Genius is not a matter of flipping a switch from dull to brilliant. That's why so few people get to experience that elusive, full-hearted, fully expressed version of their best. Before, when strength and success didn't come quickly and easily, they thought their efforts were failing, and they gave up. To be specific, they gave up on themselves. If this scenario sounds familiar to you, I'm here to let you know that it doesn't have to be this way.

Genius is there in each of us, just like an oak tree exists in every acorn. The seed grows more easily when you cultivate it steadily and don't just expect it to grow. Knowing that the seed must be nurtured in order to become a tree is key. That's the Mastery Mindset.

The genius that exists in you is always greater than the genius you believe you have. The predictable outcome of applying your Mastery Mindset is that you'll discover the best of yourself exceeds what you'd imagined possible.

Beware: You'll be an outlier. Cultivating a Mastery Mindset is counter-cultural. It's become "normal" in the modern culture to favor shiny objects with quick pay-offs over long-term satisfaction: quarterly earnings over long-term opportunities, sound bites over deeper thought, and high-volume thrills over quiet repetition.

Keeping your Mastery Mindset alive over the long term is far more challenging in today's endorphin-craving world. And the peer pressure to join the cool kids on the short-term thrill ride is as real today as it was in high school when your friends were tempting you with trouble.

The chapters in this section give insight into the Mastery Mindset. I hope these stories will expand your understanding and inspire you to dedicate yourself more deeply to it in service of your biggest dreams and your fully expressed self.

1

THE MASTERY PATH: ALWAYS AVAILABLE, NEVER CROWDED

There are no traffic jams on the road to mastery.

Look around. When you dedicate yourself to doing brilliant work and being your best, many people you know are going to fall away as you progress. They took an earlier exit at "good enough" or "I don't have time for this."

Who are Kobe Bryant's or Serena Williams' peers? Who can Elon Musk confide in who really gets him? Who really gets Warren Buffett?

The further you travel toward mastery, the less crowded is the road.

Look around this week. How many others are on this path with you?

But wait a minute... Something strange always happens...

Interestingly, the achievement of mastery isn't evenly distributed throughout the world. It exists in concentrated pockets.

Brazil produces an unfair number of soccer stars. Motown produced a disproportionate number of hits. Duke wins too many men's basketball titles to be fair. Tesla produces better cars than is reasonably predictable.

Mastery is a choice, and it starts with a commitment, an attitude.

It takes just one person to choose it. Others who are "mastery curious" take note, and a few join in.

There's often a leader on hand, a firebrand who may not say much but who knows the route to mastery.

Most people will roll their eyes and opt out. Remember, no traffic jams. But a handful put their heads down and quietly start doing the difficult work.

Why not you?

Why can't you be the one who starts it all? For your team, for your department, for your company or family?

Maybe you already have. Or if someone else has already started, why not be the next to join in?

Either you or your competitor is going to make this commitment to mastery and enjoy disproportionate success. Why not you?

Beware of false idols...

Don't be impressed by the noise and bravado from some folks. People become champions by doing the hard work when no one else is watching.

If someone boasts about how hard they're working, they're probably not on the mastery path. They're on the "look at me" path. They'll eliminate themselves eventually. You just keep going.

The overnight success?

The media loves overnight successes. There is no such thing.

There are overnight flashes in the pan. But the ones who have stayed at the top longer than five minutes traveled the same path as you for years and years before you ever knew their names.

Have some faith in the path you've chosen, and keep doing your good work. Mastery is a choice you make every day.

Head for the open road.

2

A LOVE SONG GONE WRONG: WHAT SONG IS RUNNING YOUR DREAMS?

Today, José is a thriving college graduate and a dear friend, one of the most wise and resilient people I know. He was once a Little Brother I mentored. I share his story with full permission.

We met when José was 12.

He could barely read or do math. He had just started selling drugs in a gang.

But those challenges were minimal compared to what almost destroyed him: the **Mexican love song.**

Just as José began his freshman year in high school, he fell in love for the first time.

A girl who was a junior took an interest in him. It was crazy, amazing love.

He quickly realized that she was the most beautiful woman in the world and that they would be together until death. That is, until she unceremoniously dumped him a few weeks later.

At first, José was disappointed but not devastated. Tragedy averted.

Then, things took a bad turn.

His disappointment morphed into despair and anger. He railed against her obvious betrayal, lies, and deceit.

"She never loved me!"

"She lied to me all along." "My mom knew she would betray me."

His suffering far outlasted the length of the actual relationship. His despair dwarfed his previous joy.

As I listened closely to José, the words of heartache and betrayal sounded oddly familiar—like words I'd heard before. But from where...?

Finally, it hit me.

His words reminded me of some of the popular love songs I'd heard when I worked in Latin America. In those songs, particularly Ranchera music from Mexico, love could be blissful. But love was also oh-so-torturous.

I asked him, "Bro. Have you been listening to Mexican love songs?"

His eyes opened wide with disbelief, and he exclaimed, "How did you know that?!"

"Because you sound like one. You've got to stop listening to them. They've possessed you."

He did stop.

And within two weeks, he was a new José. Heart healed. Back to full energy and focus. A normal kid.

True story.

This isn't an indictment of Mexican music.

That's the music José likes, and every culture has its heartbreak songs. (Thank you, Adele.)

Love songs aren't just songs.

Songs reshape our minds with lyrics and melodies that evoke vivid pictures and deep emotions. If you listen to them repeatedly, they're like subtle mind-control devices.

The "reality" of your song becomes your new reality, and you begin to think and act as if that reality were true.

José had been swept into a new reality that guided his decisions, words, and actions.

What is the song you play in your head?

Is it a Mexican love song? A military march? A song of resilience, strength, and mastery?

The stories you tell yourself (a.k.a. lyrics) and the mood/attitude you're feeling (a.k.a. melody) are mind control-devices that drive your decisions, actions, and behaviors, just like the love songs did to José. They determine your dreams.

José had an easy fix.

His songs were external, so he could just stop listening to them.

For the rest of us, it's much more subtle.

We don't recognize music and lyrics in our head as "songs." We call them "reality," and we keep listening. But those internal songs you're playing control your mind just like José's Mexican love songs did his.

If you're not happy with the way things are going in your world, it's time to change your song. You're the DJ of your life. Would it help to spin a few more songs of mastery and meaning?

What songs are playing in your head? Are they getting you where you want to go?

3

WHEN MY CAB BECAME A CLASSROOM IN MASTERY

Teachers appear when you need them. Rarely do they take on the form you were expecting.

My cab driver to BWI airport turned out to be a Yoda with dreadlocks. His name is Naod. I was strangely sad we didn't hit more traffic because the ride and the conversation ended too quickly.

From the back seat, I could only see his eyes and his long dreadlocks in the rearview mirror. I detected a slight accent in his speech.

So, I asked, "Where are you from, originally?"

"I'm from Ethiopia."

"Cool. How long have you been here?"

"12 years."

"Did you speak English before you came to the US?"

"No, I taught myself when I arrived."

"No way! You have almost no accent, and your English is impeccable. How'd you do that?"

Naod replied, *"To learn something, don't be shy. Today, you make a mistake. Tomorrow, you do better."*

Bam! With just 15 words, he dispensed a pearl of wisdom bigger than the Hope Diamond.

I grabbed my phone and wrote it down before I lost it.

He gave me permission to share it.

Naod kicked open a conversation that anyone with a burning desire to change the world needs to consider.

What's the most audacious, valuable thing you want to accomplish, to contribute?

If it's really audacious, you are far from achieving it now. That's why it's audacious.

At this moment, there are many, many, many things you don't know how to do to make your audacious contribution.

You have so much to learn.

So did Naod when he arrived in the US. Learning a new language was just a part of his challenge, no doubt.

In two short sentences, he illuminated how the most successful among us bridge *that wide and treacherous gap between dreaming big and delivering big:*

The people who make the greatest contributions are the greatest learners. Period.

For example, did you know Elon Musk knew nothing about rocket propulsion in 2001? He'd been working in financial services (at PayPal) before that. He founded SpaceX in 2002. You know the rest.

Let me repeat: *He knew nothing.* Then, he taught himself. If you haven't noticed, he's been changing the world, surpassing the most established companies in every field his businesses have entered. He learns better.

Madonna couldn't play an instrument or sing when she moved to New York as a college dropout. She got to learning. After a little time and a lot of ridicule, she became the most successful artist of her era. Artists today still admit to copying her style.

The gap between you and your audacious goals is simple: knowledge.

The vehicle that will get you there is equally simple: learning.

But will you ride a rocket of learning like Naod, Elon Musk, and Madonna? Or is your learning vehicle more slow and safe, like a minivan in the right-hand lane?

Learning at rocket speed is risky.

You could crash. Actually, you *will* crash. Repeatedly.

You could look stupid and clunky in front of friends and peers. Correction: You *will* look stupid and clunky.

The biggest enemy of learning is not IQ. It's not the quality of the teacher.

It's the unwillingness of the student to be a complete know-nothing-failure over and over and over.

It's avoiding the discomfort of your absolute ignorance, being unwilling to keep doing the tedious, mundane learning work with curiosity in spite of it.

It's the need to look good instead of looking stupid. Or as Green Beret Lt. Colonel (retired) Scott Mann says: Cool is the enemy of great.

Thomas Edison, one of the greatest inventors of all time, *wanted* to fail. He viewed every failure as one step closer to success. When asked about his many failed attempts to invent the lightbulb, he famously replied, "I have not failed. I've just found 10,000 ways that won't work."

How badly do you want to contribute? How important is your audacious goal?

Are you willing to do what it takes to learn at rocket speed?

Are you willing to keep trying after certain, repeated failures?

Are you willing to look stupid and awkward in front of people whose respect you want?

Where and how do you want to contribute above all else?

To paraphrase a wise man in dreadlocks, if you really want this, strap on your rocket boosters and prepare to crash.

4

MASTERY: WHAT ARE YOU WILLING TO DO WHEN NO ONE IS WATCHING?

By the end of any January, upwards of 80% of people have fallen behind or given up on their New Year's resolutions to be better.

Why people fail or succeed is mostly about what they're willing to do when no one is watching.

New Year's resolutions are simply a magnified and accelerated version of how people succeed or fail all of the time.

Truthfully, most people and teams fail to achieve their big-stretch goals—at least the first time. Otherwise, it wouldn't be a stretch. Knowing how to stay in the game anyway gives you a great advantage.

What does the successful minority do differently?

Anson Dorrance knows a lot about success. As head coach of the University of North Carolina's women's soccer team, his teams have won 21 of the possible 31 NCAA Women's Soccer Championships that have ever been won.

That's a ridiculous accomplishment. And it's worth paying attention to.

He said, *"The vision of a champion is someone who is bent over, drenched in sweat, at the point of exhaustion when no one else is watching."*

Every person you know who is the best at what they do is living some version of this. It's not a secret. It's just that they were alone, so no one saw them traveling the mastery path.

What do you do when no one is watching?

This isn't just about working long hours. That can be a terrible waste of time. It's about being strategic about where and how you do your work.

Here are three questions to help you make your best strategic choices:

- What courageous goal are you absolutely committed to?
- What skills, abilities, and qualities must you possess to achieve that goal (i.e., what power do you need)?
- What do you need to practice repeatedly, even when no one knows you're doing it, to build that power in yourself?

This is not about eating your vegetables or suffering for its own sake.

Yes, stretching will be frustrating, tedious, or excruciating, regularly. Strangely, doing the hard work when you're all alone also becomes comforting, even therapeutic. It becomes a security blanket, and it boosts your feelings of confidence. It helps you find your imaginary limits and experience the thrill of busting them. It gives you "go-to moves" that make you feel powerful when you need to. It builds your resilience.

Anyone can work hard because the boss told them to.

Champions in any field are quietly developing their power while no one is watching, when no one asked.

5

A CHAMPION COACH SCHOOLS US IN HOW TO BUILD A TALENT HOTBED

What's it take to build a dynasty?

A good friend of mine named Sarah (or "Ms. Reck" to her students) recently directed her final band concert after 32 years of teaching high school band.

She was a maestro at building a talent hotbed, a place where great talent is disproportionately concentrated. Cultivated over time, talent hotbeds can grow into dynasties.

Her mastery applies far beyond teaching… so pay attention, students!

Sarah reluctantly agreed to let me write about her work so we can all learn. Confession: to get her agreement, I might have failed to mention I'd use the words "talent hotbed" and "dynasty." Forgive me, Ms. Reck!

First, some stats:

Ms. Reck taught her final 27 years at Ottawa Township High School (OTHS) in North Central Illinois. She had 892 students in total.

Get this! The combined OTHS bands and choirs swept the Illinois High School Association State Music Sweepstakes *20 years in a row*, winning 21 times in total. To put that in perspective:

- The OTHS Music Department holds the 11 highest scores in the competition's 44-year history.

- The state's second winningest school music program placed first eight times.

- The second most consecutive wins by another high school was five.

Sit up straight, and let this teacher school us today.

I've marveled at Sarah's success for years. But during her final concert, as her current and former students stepped to the mic to share their experiences, they gave us a peek into her approach.

How well do you cultivate talent as a leader?

Her students offered great insights into how to create an impact much bigger than yourself. As you read them, look in the mirror and ask yourself how you're leading in these areas.

Ms. Reck was a teacher first.

Her goal was to get students to produce the best possible music, and she made it her job to teach them how, including asking for help from other pros to achieve that goal. She was willing to bring in tutors and mentors who knew more about something than she did. It was about developing her students' talent, not about knowing it all.

No one said she didn't *like* being first! But winning was just the cherry on top. Cultivating the best in her students was the primo goal.

The moral of the story: *Dynasty-builders focus on making others great.* You can create a flash in the pan if you try to be the hero and save the day personally. You create a talent hotbed by making everyone around you exceptionally strong. If you do it for years, you build a dynasty.

Three moves she made to help others be strong were:

- **Don't let the bar stop rising.** Students spoke of how she kept raising the bar for their performance. She let them know directly when they'd cleared it and when they'd fallen short. She also kept raising the bar for her own teaching.

- **People, then performance.** Every student spoke of the personal interest she took in them being their best—as people and as musicians—even after graduation. They wanted to perform at a higher level because they knew she was backing them personally.

- **Prepare, prepare, prepare.** Students knew Ms. Reck expected them to keep doing the work even when she wasn't watching. Bobby Knight captured her ethos with his quote: "Most people have the will to win, few have the will to prepare to win." She inspired them to do the work.

I pity the poor school that wants to unseat OTHS.

By focusing on the right things year after year, they've made themselves tough to touch.

Building a dynasty wasn't the goal. It was the result of years of great leadership and great work.

What about you? How are you building a talent hotbed?

6
HOW A VIRTUOSO VIEWS TIME DIFFERENTLY

Recently, I had the chance to have a brief conversation with celebrated Pulitzer Prize-winning author, Ron Chernow.

He made a comment that rang a bell in my head. It will no doubt be valuable for you too if you intend to make a meaningful impact in your world.

He's a true virtuoso.

Chernow is best known for writing the book *Alexander Hamilton*. Every book he writes is an award winner. Chernow's biography, *Alexander Hamilton*, inspired Lin-Manuel Miranda to write the earth-shaking musical named *Hamilton*.

And that would be enough.

But he also published books in 1990, 1994, 1997, 1998, 2004, 2010, and 2017.

He has a reputation for painstaking research that helps him tell the stories of influential, complicated people who've made a great impact in the world. His biographies seem to dispel myths and inject more truth and humanity into their stories.

He doesn't take the easy route.

He's very serious about producing good work. I'm still making my way through two of his very thick but engaging books.

At a recent book signing event, my wife Brenda and I were the last people in the line to get our books signed. With no one waiting behind us, he was able to spend a few minutes chatting with us.

I wondered what his writing experience was like.

Because it's taking me a long time to read his books, I asked him, "How many hours does it take you to complete a biography?" I expected him to give me a number in the thousands.

He seemed surprised by the question.

He cocked his head thoughtfully and said, "Hours? Wow, I don't think of it in hours. It's more like YEARS."

Bam! And that's why he's a master.

How often do you set a goal that will take you years to achieve?

For most of us in this fast-paced world, goals are measured in weeks or quarters, maybe a year. Other than raising your kids well, how many goals have you set that you're willing to devote years to?

In most parts of our modern world, people would think you were odd if you talked about a goal that will take you five or ten years to achieve.

Fast is not bad. It's just not all there is.

The "show me the money NOW!" mindset that drives much of our fast-paced world will definitely produce some great things quickly. Yet, it limits us from taking on some longer-term endeavors that may have a greater impact on the world—and have more meaning to you.

He's leveraging the Mastery Mindset.

Chernow is going counter-culture with his Mastery Mindset, which often measures success in years or even decades.

He's willing to bite off a huge goal knowing that he'll have nothing to show for it in a week or in a year. And still, he comes back to the mostly solitary work with enthusiasm—week after week, book after book.

He's willing to endure years of what you'll always encounter on a long journey: setbacks, roadblocks, dead ends, criticism, confusion, frustration, doubt, fear, boredom, aging.

Sometimes, it's not about you.

When you pick a goal so far away, others may actually receive more for your efforts than you will.

Outliers inspire.

Who are the people you respect for their contributions to the world? It's likely they're thinking in terms of years or decades for their goals too. They're not normal.

They are the outliers: The people making disproportionate and impactful contributions to their world.

For example…

A retired forester I'm lucky to know, Rex Mann, has a goal to restore the American Chestnut tree, which was wiped out to extinction by blight in the 20th century. The four billion thriving American Chestnut trees that once dominated the eastern half of the U.S. were a critical puzzle piece of the ecosystem. Restoring it would be a positive game changer.

However, Rex doesn't expect to see the tree restored in his lifetime. He hopes his grandkids will enjoy it. Still, he toils away for hours a day on behalf of this goal he'll never experience himself.

Ordinary people with a long-term view can do extraordinary things.

Neil Armstrong was the first human to walk on the moon at age 38. His sacrifices to achieve that feat benefited and inspired billions of people he never met. He grew up as an ordinary kid in small Ohio towns. But he pursued his dream for decades. He got his pilot's license at 16 and kept pushing frontiers in flight for years even after his historic moon walk.

Embracing the Mastery Mindset is counter-cultural.

Everywhere you turn—at work, on TV or the internet, in your neighborhood, you're surrounded by a culture that prizes speed, novelty, and quick gratification.

Yet, some of the most valuable goals take time. Years. And years. Or even decades.

It's not that the goal is to take a long time to achieve your objectives. It's just that taking on the Mastery Mindset means you're WILLING to dedicate yourself to a long run to get there.

What about you? What are you willing to devote years to building? To deliver on what your generous heart wants to create, you'll need a <u>Mastery Mindset</u>. Often, you'll find yourself alone on the long journey. Along the way, you'll also find compatriots—other outliers—on their own multi-year mastery paths.

Perhaps it's self-selection, but I'd imagine that every person Chernow's written about also possessed that long-term Mastery Mindset.

So, what about you?

What are the most meaningful contributions you wish to make? How long are you willing to work at it?

7

THROUGH THE EYES OF A MASTER

In November 2013, I spent 10 days in Nepal trekking in the Himalayan Mountains. There were no paved roads above 10,000 feet, which meant no motorized vehicles.

Without our typical noise and distractions, we can find atypical insights.

It was just silence and the unfamiliar.

Beneath the quiet sky, we ascended, descended, and ascended more for hours each day. Around every turn was more wind, sun, and endless ranges of jagged peaks shooting toward the heavens.

We were led by a sherpa guide named Lakpa.

Lakpa was a master of his mountains. He knew the landscape down to the individual stones on the path. Without him, it'd have been something between a frustrating hike and a dangerous struggle. With him, it was an adventure, even a pilgrimage.

Lakpa saw what we could not. He saw that we were doing something bigger than just climbing a mountain. With his bare eyes, he spied a rare snow leopard as it hunted mountain goats far away on the next mountainside.

We saw nothing.

He shouted and pointed excitedly, "Loooook! Loooook! Loooook!" We needed binoculars to recognize the speck he was pointing to. We were in awe of what we saw.

Lakpa knew the dangers.

Sometimes, I'd try to climb an incline too quickly in the thin air. Before I was aware of my error, Lakpa would have already appeared behind me out of nowhere to gently instruct, "slow, slow" in my ear.

A master guide made all the difference.

Lakpa knew the terrain and the surroundings, having traveled it many times. He brought the mountains and the people and the paths to life in a way none of us could have imagined on our own.

It sounds cliché, but that journey changed my life. After he showed us his world, I saw my world anew.

It's the classic combination for transformation anyone can use:

- **unfamiliar territory, and**
- **a knowledgeable guide.**

It's such a classic 1-2 combo, it's in our favorite stories. The combination created some pretty remarkable results for Luke Skywalker with Yoda and for Frodo Baggins with Gandalf as they faced unyielding challenges.

And it's worked for any person who's ever ventured beyond their former limitations—like you.

Sometimes, you choose the challenge—like I chose my trek.

Sometimes, it chooses you.

Either way, the opportunity to be transformed is there. Especially with a guide who knows the territory well.

Your world may not change, but you'll never experience your world the same after living the challenge.

What's your perspective?

Life or work might be twisting you like a pretzel right now, and it may feel full of daunting challenges.

Are you making it a struggle? Or do you understand this is the threshold to your transformation? If you play along and stop resisting, that is.

It's easier to understand there's a breakthrough coming when you're hiking with a guide in Nepal or watching a movie you know will end well.

It's more difficult to trust in a breakthrough when it's real life and the stakes are high.

But in every messy situation, the possibility is still there, especially with good guidance.

Is something kicking your butt right now?

While your struggle may feel unusual and unique to you, you're reliving a pattern as old as humankind. It's the challenge and the inherent possibility of wisdom and strength.

Are you fighting it or flowing with it? (Hint: "Use the Force, Luke." Lean into what's possible.) And find your Lakpa, someone who knows this territory better than you to give you guidance.

8

RETHINKING YOUR SOURCES OF WISDOM

I sat and listened intently as my mentor shared some pretty amazing wisdom with me. His perspective and experiences were so different than mine that I needed to stop him every few minutes and ask for clarification.

Not everything he said made sense, but parts of what he shared were exploding in my brain. I'd just never thought of things the way he was describing them.

Have you ever had one of those moments when someone quietly revealed to you a world you'd never known?

My mentor and I both finished our cups of hot chocolate. Then, I threw down my credit card and paid for them.

I didn't buy because he'd been teaching me.

It was because he didn't have much money. He was 17.

Especially in the last decade, I've taken on many more young teachers and mentors. As you get older, you may also find your universe of potential teachers is expanding.

A couple of months ago, I got schooled in life by a 6-year-old. I thought I was teaching her to throw a Frisbee, but by the time she had mastered her wrist flip, I was also viewing the world differently.

And a few years before that, a 30-something playwright taught me as much about life as many grey-haired adults did with his Broadway musical *Hamilton*. You may also appreciate this goofy 16-year old in Chapter 36 who is teaching anyone who's watching about resilience.

Who will you let mentor you?

The paradigm I'd been raised in was that mentors were supposed to be older and more experienced. The ignorance of youth hopefully becomes the wisdom of maturity.

But as the physicist and Nobel Prize winner Niels Bohr once said, "… the opposite of one profound truth may very well be another profound truth." In other words, there is tremendous wisdom in youth.

No, I'm not suggesting you buy everything your younger friends tell you any more than I believe you should listen to everything your elders say. Yet, there are threads of wisdom in surprising places if you're willing to pay attention.

I will still seek advice from those older people who have traveled more miles than I have when I'm at life's critical junctures. But without the fresh wisdom of youth, I think I'd have already crashed my life into the ditch by now. Or I'd be bored out of my mind.

How about you?

Who are you willing to let teach you? One of your roles on your Mastery Path is being creative and sometimes uncomfortable with your choice of teachers.

For me, the ideal mentoring relationship is someone who both can teach me and is willing to learn from me. No single one of us can see it all, but I want to hang out with the people who are paying deep attention to their world, regardless of age or status.

The world is your schoolyard, but the people you'll learn from aren't always the ones who are labeled as teachers.

Look around. There is wisdom in your midst.

● SECTION II:

YOUR DREAMS: POSSIBILITIES THAT TAKE HOLD OF YOUR HEART

Some thoughts and feelings just won't leave you alone. They inspire you. They might even scare you because they're so important or they feel far out of reach. You can try to turn away from them, but they find you again and again. That's because they live deep in you, so no matter where you go, they're always there, waiting for you.

Those are your dreams. Inspiring, frustrating, invigorating dreams.

Your genius is directly connected to your dreams. To bring those dreams to life, you must awaken more of your genius. Some people pursue big dreams as their way of forcing themselves to express more of their genius.

Look back on dreams you've already achieved. Haven't you found that the experience of expanding your brilliance to achieve your dream is often as satisfying as achieving the dream itself? Sometimes, even more so.

There will be times when you're not consciously aware you have a new dream. But already, it's calling out your best. You'll look back later and realize it was calling you forward to do something or be someone before you even had words to describe it.

 go to www.davidmartinco.com/ftg-videos

Some people work hard not to let themselves dream. The potential risk and disappointment of not living their dream is too great, so they do their best to shut down their dreams. In the process, they also cut themselves off from being inspired and engaged.

But dreaming is as essential to being human as breathing is. You can't stop it.

What's your experience? You probably have some dreams that are holding onto your heart right now. Are you allowing them to light you up? Are you foolish enough (in a good way) to actually believe you could achieve them?

This section offers examples and advice meant to both inspire you and guide you to cultivate those dreams that are calling you. To bring those dreams to life, you'll be forced to free more of your genius-self to make it happen. Keep dreaming.

9

HE IMITATED HIS WAY TO HIS DREAM—AND SO CAN YOU

Willson Contreras, the 26-year-old catcher for the Chicago Cubs, played in his first All-Star game in July 2018. That's one of the biggest honors in his profession.

When he found out he'd made the team, he cried.

You probably would have cried too if you'd have worked that hard—especially if one of your idols had tried to hold you in place as you'd started gaining ground.

Regardless, you can steal his path to All-Star status starting today. And perhaps your success will threaten some of your idols as well.

Playing in the All-Star game was a predictable outcome.

Contreras used a method that almost every superstar or top performer in any field, including business, has used since the beginning of humanity.

He knew where to focus.

It wasn't long ago that Contreras was just a pimply-faced teenager with a dream. Wisely, he found a secret weapon: his idols.

In particular, he idolized two big league catchers: Buster Posey (San Francisco Giants) and Yadi Molina (St. Louis Cardinals). When Contreras was a kid, Posey and Molina were two future Hall of Fame catchers at the peak of their game.

Contreras focused on them. He studied their moves in minute, painful detail. He practiced doing what they did as closely as he could, day after day after day.

He imitated them until he could make those moves as well as (or better than) they did.

How do I know this?

Because that's what every person who's having a huge impact will tell you he or she did early on.

- Kobe Bryant studied Michael Jordan move by move.
- Babe Ruth studied Shoeless Joe Jackson swing by swing.
- Lin-Manuel Miranda wrote down the lyrics of Stephen Sondheim and hip-hop artists word by word.
- Warren Buffett read (and still reads) to capture the genius of great thinkers, idea by idea.
- The Founding Fathers of the US researched the masters of history, thesis by thesis, to the point where they'd sometimes memorized their words.

And over time, each of them began to perform those things in their way. Not as clones but as their own original expressions.

There's even an advantage to birth order.

Did you know that the vast majority of Olympians fall toward the bottom of their family's birth order? As a younger, smaller, slower sibling, they had to work harder to keep up with their older siblings. So they imitated them.

Imitation was a survival skill with Olympic-sized benefits. It made them better, faster.

In fact, it's not uncommon for a dedicated student to eventually outperform the people they'd been imitating.

Stealing talent is legal and encouraged.

Daniel Coyle, the author of *The Talent Code: Greatness Isn't Born. It's Grown. Here's How.* (a must-read for anyone who wants to have a disproportionate impact), calls it "windshield time"—keeping the people you want to emulate right in front of you—in your windshield.

Contreras never became his heroes.

That wasn't his goal. Contreras would be a terrible Buster Posey. But by mastering Posey's moves, he became much better himself.

As proof, Contreras hit a home run on the first pitch thrown to him in the All-Star game. When you know his story, are you surprised?

His idol tried to smack him down.

In 2017, Contreras admitted to studying Posey and Molina... and then added that he hopes to surpass them. The next day, Molina smacked him down on Twitter, essentially telling him to "respect the ranks." But it was too late. Contreras was on his way.

So today, ask yourself two questions:

- *Who might have put YOU on their windshield?*

  The likelihood is that they will eventually surpass you. You can choose to support their progress or smack them down. Played well, they could become a part of the legacy you leave.

- *Who are you putting on your windshield? Who do you want to emulate?*

  Get clear about who it is, and start imitating them shamelessly. If you're dedicated to the task, it will make you a better version of yourself.

Want to make a meaningful impact? Put your idols on your windshield, and get to work.

10

SOME DREAMERS CREATE THEIR OWN MIRACLES: LESSON 1

What could you have in common with a junior high flunkee?

At 12, José was failing in school. He couldn't read, write, or do math. Not just sort of. Not at all.

He was living in a dangerous neighborhood and trying to be the man of the house. His father had abandoned his family (mom, José, and two younger sisters) when José was eight, and they struggled in extreme poverty.

People predicted his failure.

José's eighth-grade math teacher told him he'd never graduate high school.

A doctor suggested that José's difficult birth might have caused "brain damage." His mom should just accept José wasn't going to get better.

Then, José embarked an 11-year self-induced miracle.

José decided he didn't like the stories others were telling him about his future, and he chose a new one.

In May 2018, he took the next step in his miraculous journey. He received his undergraduate diploma from Xavier University. Then, he moved to DC to lobby Congress for immigration reform.

You're more like José than you might think.

Don't be deceived by the external circumstances. The principles José applied to create his miracle are relevant to anyone who hopes there is a dream still unlived in them.

What's the better version of you waiting for a miracle?

José still teaches me about the limitless depth of the human spirit and the true meaning of grit. Why not apply José's lessons to create your own miracles?

Miracle: A possibility that exists beyond your belief of what could be. (In other words, miracles aren't magic. They're just hard to believe.)

I had a front-row seat to this miracle. José was my Little Brother in the Big Brothers Big Sisters program.

Something started happening: a new story that fueled a miracle.

As José told others what he was trying to do, people started stepping up for him in miraculous ways. Almost out of thin air, random people started offering tutoring, guidance, connections, sometimes even money.

It happened so often that I gave it a name: *Equipo José (Team José)*. It does take a village, and José attracted his just as you can.

Lessons from a flunkee:

Here are two of many lessons I learned from watching José. Please steal them shamelessly.

1. People can't resist an underdog who's putting in the work.
2. Mind over matter is not just a cliché.

I'll write about Lesson 1 here and about Lesson 2 in the next chapter.

Lesson #1: People can't resist an underdog who's doing the work. Why?

Nothing is more intoxicating for humans than to live our own lives full-out and fully expressed... yet, it's surprisingly difficult to do. There are so many things that stop us, mostly self-created. (See Section III of this book for more stories about feeling alive.)

Therefore, when we do encounter someone who is truly going for it without caution in spite of terrible odds, we are drawn to them.

Vitality is magnetic.

We know it in our gut.

Being around a person who is living in a fully expressed way stirs something in us to come to life, and we like that feeling.

(Caveat: José had plenty of detractors along the way, most of whom were close to him—even his relatives. He started defying their pre-formed small, negative images of him. Perhaps his unlikely blips of success revealed that they'd given up on themselves too soon? Perhaps they were thinking, "Get back in your box, young man! Your success is making me realize I sold myself short.")

How can you attract miraculous levels of support?

There are two factors that seemed to influence people's attraction to José. You'll need both of these to draw support for your big dreams.

Factor A: How extreme is your stretch?

As the likelihood of success nears "impossible," support grows exponentially.

José's stretch goal wasn't just to learn to read. He wanted to become the Martin Luther King, Jr. of immigration reform.

Ridiculous, right? Or is it *ridiculously inspiring* to know someone who dreams that big, not just for himself but also to help others?

We are drawn to people who are borderline naive about their chances for success but who still stay committed.

One of Steve Jobs' greatest gifts was what people called his "reality distortion field." In spite of common sense, he believed ridiculous things were possible. Meanwhile, the people close to Jobs often wanted to throttle him.

Yet, there are few who could light up the human spirit like he could.

Jobs wasn't just pushing the frontiers of technology. He was generously reminding all of us of our own limitless potential by brazenly looking beyond "accepted" limitations. *That* is attractive.

Factor B: How hard are you working for it?

You know plenty of big dreamers who tell you they're going to change the world... as they stuff their faces with Cheetos and binge-watch *Friends* reruns.

What differentiated José from the other 99% was the fact that he backed it up with hard work.

In addition to playing the demanding "man of the house" role to look out for his family as his culture expected of him, he worked hard—before, after, and in between—to hone his skills as a student, storyteller, advocate, and lobbyist.

As people began to see how hard this dreamer was working, *Equipo José* began to materialize.

Sometimes, people who'd just met him volunteered their support. At a deep level, he was reminding them of their own limitless potential. And that was worth investing in.

I am one of those people he drew in. I love a good underdog. Don't you?

Whiners don't draw us in.

When I first met José, he told a "poor me" story about his tough lot in life. No one was impressed.

Eventually, inspired by his mom's tenacity to fight against the odds, his story morphed into: "I've got big work to do."

Then, he backed it up with hard work. *That* was when the supporters started showing up.

Now, it's your turn to live bigger and brighter.

How can you apply José's teachings today?

Applying Factor A: What's the big stretch you're sitting on? Your ridiculous, generous dream?

If it's big, it's going to be something you're almost embarrassed to say out loud.

I got José's permission to share his dream about becoming the MLK, Jr. of immigration reform, but until today, he's never shared that with more than three or four people. It was too embarrassing and too precious. He let me share it to inspire you.

Remember this: Even if you never realize your ridiculous dream in your lifetime, doesn't it wake something up in you to try? And couldn't your act of stretching awaken people around you to the best in themselves also?

So, what is it for you? What is your ridiculous dream?

If you feel fear, embarrassment, or anxiety as you imagine it, you're probably on the right track. Guard it closely, because you'll have plenty of detractors. But why not declare it to yourself?

Applying Factor B: What is the hard work no one else will do to achieve this? Will you do the work every day?

Dreaming big is hard enough. Doing the work to make those dreams come to life is much harder because you have to stick with it day after day. On most days, you'll see zero progress or worse. But you keep doing the work.

99% of people fall out at this step. The remaining 1% possess no special qualities except for a plan to implement and a higher tolerance for pain. They just keep doing the uncomfortable, boring, humiliating work anyway.

What uncomfortable actions will you take to bring your dream to life? How and when will you begin?

There's nothing in José's story that doesn't and can't apply to you. Take a moment and consider where and how you can apply his approach to live your own impossible dreams. They WILL be impossible until you begin.

11

WHAT I LEARNED FROM AN ILLITERATE DREAMER: LESSON 2

In Chapter 10, you met José. If you haven't read his story and the lessons he teaches all of us, I'd recommend it.

José couldn't read, write, or do math when he was 12. In May 2018, he graduated from Xavier University ready to change the world.

And he will. After all, he's developed a secret power.

Few people will overcome odds like José did. But it's very possible to do.

Will you apply José's secret powers to make your own miracles?

It helps to have an inspiring reason to develop those powers.

What would wild, meaningful success look like for you? In those brief moments of quiet when your attention isn't flooded with noise, activity, and distraction, what bigger dream stirs within you?

In the last chapter, I shared **two key lessons** I've learned from watching José recreate himself.

1. People can't resist an underdog who's doing the work. We went deep on this lesson in the last chapter. (See Section IV of this book for more about cultivating the underdog in you.)

2. Mind over matter is not just a cliché.

This chapter is about how you can apply the second lesson, starting today.

Who are you taking advice from?

As a teenager, José recognized that there was an enormous obstacle (or superpower, if applied wisely) within him. You have it too.

It's right under all of our noses, yet unless you have a trained eye, it's completely invisible.

It's like a secret power in you that can be developed for good or evil.

It is: How you talk TO yourself ABOUT yourself.

All day long, you have a running conversation in your head, assessing and explaining your past, present, and future life experiences. Everyone does.

Yet, it's so constant and so common among all of us that it's like breathing. We aren't fully conscious of this talking. It's just there.

Still, we're *always* listening—whether our thoughts are wise or uninformed, courageous or fearful.

Most of us believe what we think.

But if you want to do bigger work in the world, believing everything you think can be a limiting and dangerous practice.

If all of this sounds like nonsense to you, 12-year-old José thought so too. Now, he uses this knowledge as his Miracle-Making Machine.

Change your conversation. Change your world.

Over the past 11 years, how José talks to himself about himself has completely changed. As a result, so has his world. Cause and effect. Mind over matter.

Most people flip the cause and effect.

We're taught early in life that our thoughts are a reaction to our world. When something good happens (cause), we think happy thoughts (effect). When something bad happens (cause), we think unhappy thoughts (effect). It's simple and easy to understand.

And it's wrong.

If you want to create a miracle, you can't wait until things go well to start thinking better.

That's the secret power: You can learn to manage what and how you think, regardless of what the outside world brings you.

There is a cause and effect. It's just opposite of what you were taught.

If you want to create your own miracles, you must change the way you think and talk to yourself now. Then, your world will begin to change.

Many people were entertained by the story in Chapter 2, "A Love Song Gone Wrong," where José's thoughts took him down a rabbit hole of lovesick misery. Yet, the insights he gained from pulling himself out of the rabbit hole fueled much of the change that followed.

Here's a summary of the progression of José's cause and effect. This is his progression of mind over matter.

Age	Cause: Thoughts about himself	Effect: Outcomes in his life
12	"I'm dumb. I'm stupid."	José couldn't read, write, or do math. He didn't try.
15	"Maybe I'm not stupid."	José began to make an effort in school. He stopped failing classes.
16	"Maybe I'm smart, but I learn differently."	José earned honors his freshman through senior years. José began speaking in large groups about immigration reform.
18	I am smart. I really am smart.	José applied to college.
19	I am highly favored and truly blessed. (José adapted this phrase from motivational speaker Les Brown as his new mantra.)	José was accepted to Xavier University. He struggled in his freshman and sophomore years but never quit. José held a job throughout college and continued to tell his story to large crowds. José began to lobby in Congress.

When José started talking to himself differently, he had no idea where things would end up. He just knew how he talked to himself was something that was in his control.

Each phase of change makes the next phase possible.

He could never have considered adopting Les Brown's "I am highly favored and truly blessed" when he was telling himself "I'm dumb. I'm stupid." You can only see your next step, not all the steps.

What are you saying *to* yourself *about* yourself?

So, you want to change the world? Before you start telling everyone else how they need to change, follow José's lead. Change your conversation with yourself about yourself.

What is one slightly better thing you could start saying to yourself *about* yourself?

12

LET AN OLD FARMER'S WISDOM HELP YOUR DREAMS GROW

Every spring, without fail, my dad marveled at the same thing.

So did my grandpa. Their combined years in farming total over a century, so this is old-school farm-family wisdom.

The message was about timing, and it's 100% applicable to you.

In farming, you plant a seed and expect it to start growing almost immediately.

In the wild of nature, it's different. A seed that falls to the earth can lie dormant for years and never take root. Then, one day, it starts to grow.

Why then? Maybe the soil was tilled and lifted that seed to the surface. Maybe the soil and climate conditions changed. Or maybe it was just the right time.

That seed took root and started shooting toward the sky.

Stand with my dad and me as we look out across his field.

I have a memory of standing next to my dad behind our farmhouse. We were looking north over acres of short green sprouts of soybeans peeking up through fresh, rich soil. Dad is pointing out the unwelcome weeds* that had also sprouted, seemingly out of nowhere.

---

* *A weed is just a plant that grows where the farmer didn't want it!*

The farmer in him isn't so happy about the weeds.

But the dreamer in him appreciates the mysteries of nature. Every year, new weeds sprouted out of nowhere, and he marveled at that mystery.

Stand with me as we look across your field—of dreams.

You and I know you've got the seed of an audacious idea in you. A big dream.

You're human, and that means you'll always wish or dream for something better. You've got *at least* one seed of a dream in you right now.

When will it take root? That's mostly up to you. A better harvest and greater satisfaction await you.

Permission to grow.

No one gave the "weed" seeds in my dad's bean field permission to grow. They just did.

News flash: No one is going to give you permission to start growing that big, audacious dream you have either.

You just begin. You give yourself permission.

What did the people you admire do?

Think of specific people who you admire for making a great impact on their world. One thing they have in common: They gave *themselves* permission to make an impact even when their idea was just a weed to someone else.

You've already done great things. But this next big idea is probably bigger and scarier than any of them.

Maybe you should just wait. Maybe someone else will start it.

Hindsight is 20/20: Most leaders wish they'd moved sooner.

Yes, timing and patience matter. Be wise.

But most leaders who reflect back on their work say they wished they'd acted on their dream sooner.

What will you say when you look back?

Do you share their three most common reasons for waiting too long?

1. Are you waiting for someone to give you the nod of approval or permission?

2. Are you waiting for another big project to end first?

3. Are you waiting until you figure out *how* you'll reach the goal before you take the first steps?

In retrospect, they realized those three reasons were irrelevant to when to act on their new idea.

Hail to the seed that can sprout when it's told to.

But this chapter is dedicated to the seed that sprouts because it's time to.

Is now your time?

13

THIS POPULAR BUSINESS FABLE COULD KILL YOUR DREAMS... ACCIDENTALLY

A good parable helps you retain a valuable lesson for a lifetime. But what if a parable that leaders love to share is missing a critical point? Oops!

The story as it's usually told...

If you put a bunch of crabs in a bucket, eventually, one of them will climb to the top and start to escape. (Imagine that's you!)

Just as you're about to break free, another crab reaches up and pulls you back down.

The moral of the story is a warning.

If you plan to do something big, beware! People don't like it when you move up, and they'll try to hold you down.

It's a useful lesson.

It's true that some people will try to drag you down when you reach the top of the bucket.

That lesson will keep you safe, but it won't always help you succeed.

If you plan to do really big things, you need a second view of the story and the lesson it offers.

If you've successfully led a revolution in your company or in your industry, you may already know this.

A new view from *their* perspective: Why are crabs pulling at you?

In that bucket of crabs lies your future allies and advocates. Don't dismiss them too quickly.

Have you ever tried to get close to someone who's having more success than you are? Someone with wisdom and experience?

That person is on the way up (out of the bucket), and you want to learn from her.

You're reaching up—*but it's not to pull her down*. You're asking for a hand up so you can see the world from her perspective.

You may even be trying to support that crab who's found the way out. You know that'll be easier once you've viewed the world from their level.

Adjusting your view from the top of the bucket.

If you're the one at the top of the bucket right now, your grand dream is way too big to deliver by yourself.

You need many of those crabs from your bucket to join your cause. They're your future allies and advocates, *remember*?

And although it may seem like they're just clawing at you, they might just be asking for your support.

Know the whole story before you act.

If you know only the popular version of this story, you may be fighting off the very people you need to help you. Their way of reaching up may appear threatening. But maybe they just can't yet see what you do from the top of the bucket.

Yes, some of them do want to take you down. But not all of them.

If you want to lead a revolution, **your job includes pulling those people up.**

They might point out the flaws in your plan at first. They may be nervous and intimidated.

But if you kick them all back into the bucket, you just killed your revolution.

What's their story?

Are you kicking them down or pulling them up?

14

ARE YOU FIGHTING YOUR OWN DREAMS?

A wise client made a comment to me the other day. It was short and sweet, and it can help you look at yourself in the mirror in a new way.

She said, *"It's hard to fight and win against your competition when you keep fighting yourself."*

She was referring to some senior leaders in one of her divisions who had been unknowingly and unintentionally taking each other down and holding their business back from success.

How about a quick look in the mirror?

Championship sports teams, championship brands, and championship companies have at least one thing in common: **They're crystal clear about who their competition is.**

It's the *other* team. It's the *other* brand.

It's not a member of their team, the finance department (or sales or engineering), or their fellow VP.

This doesn't mean championship team members like each other and always agree. Many times, they don't get along off the court or outside the office.

But champions are smart enough to know that it's pretty hard to live their dreams—win the tournament or win in the market—if they're fighting and competing against their own team members.

Simple concept. But not easy.

Is it time for you to act?

Smart leaders help their team members stay focused on the real foe—the one on the outside. They align their efforts toward a single purpose so they will win.

They lead their teams to focus on the real foe… because the leaders of their toughest competitors are doing same thing.

Your competitors are too.

Which battles are you fighting?

The ones on the inside (with other people, other divisions, within yourself)? Or the ones in the marketplace?

If your biggest competition is not the one in the marketplace, you've got some re-thinking to do.

More importantly, you've got some leading to do.

15

FIVE QUESTIONS TO LAUNCH EVERY PROJECT: LOOK BACK TO BLAST FORWARD

Are you launching something new?

Who are the people you're counting on to deliver results? How well have you prepared them for the challenges ahead? How prepared are you?

Here are five questions you can answer together or separately to help everyone sync up quickly. It's helpful to do this as a team. Our teammates often see things we miss, both in ourselves and in the work we share.

Look backward (at the last big initiative, the last year, your last job).

What were your:

1. Triumphs/breakthroughs/wins/progresses?

    What were you proud of? What felt great to achieve? What got celebrated? What got noticed?

2. Mistakes/failures/challenges/obstacles/dead ends?

    What events or circumstances did you feel upset, angry, disappointed, or embarrassed about? What did not go as planned? What made you want to quit? What drained your energy?

3. Powers?

   Reflect on your experiences to identify the new power you have developed. Be specific. Because of your previous experiences—the successes from question 1 and the failures from question 2…

   • How am I stronger?
   • How am I smarter/wiser?
   • How am I clearer?
   • What lessons have I learned?
   • What experience did I gain that I can leverage in the future?
   • What are my new tools/abilities?
   • How am I more confident?
   • How am I more connected to myself or others?
   • How am I more free, relaxed, light, less worried/uptight?
   • What new approaches have I adopted?
   • What new connections or relationships have I formed?

Next steps:

1. Make them real.

   Naming your powers makes them seem more tangible, more substantial. (For example, you could call it a car, or you could call it a Ferrari. Which is more tangible and substantial?) If it's tangible, you'll access it more easily.

   Name your new powers just like you might in a video game (e.g., reading between the lines could be named x-ray vision, strategic thinking could be your strategy software, thinking faster becomes a superconductor, resilience could be your extra lives, deeper commitment could be dynamite, new connections could be Gorilla Glue®, more courage becomes invincibility, etc. Have some fun with them so they're memorable.)

2. Name your arena.

Where and how will you use this superpower to achieve your goal? That's your arena.

It's great to know your powers and have names for them. The ultimate step is to name the arena where you will apply them so your brain is ready when you walk into that arena.

Get specific. In what activities, on what projects, with what people, and in what situations will you access and apply these powers? And how do you plan to apply them?

If you do this with your team, replace each "I" in the questions with "we." Teams have collective powers.

Know thyself. Lead more powerfully.

With this deeper knowledge of yourself and your team, how will you carry on with this work in front of you?

Every new repetition is the next iteration of you. Keep building.

16

YOUR LEGACY: ASK ONE EXTRA QUESTION WHEN YOU START SOMETHING NEW

Something small but important happened to me one weekend. It could help you change the way you think about every new project you launch.

I drove back to my hometown in Illinois to spend some time with family. My parents' old house was empty and for sale, so I stopped by to check it out.

I was locked out.

I usually enter through the garage door, but the outside keypad had a dead battery. No luck. And all of the doors were locked.

History helped me.

Then, I remembered a conversation I'd had with my dad eight years earlier when he and my mom were moving into the house. He'd showed me where he'd hidden an extra house key in case of emergency.

I found the key and let myself in.

Legacy comes in all shapes and sizes.

My dad had died six months earlier. But I was benefitting from his intention and his actions from when he was living.

My experience is a perfect reminder of how your actions can live beyond you. And you don't have to die for this to apply!

For the people who follow you...

Every single day, you have the opportunity to leave behind some part of yourself to help the people who follow you.

You'll know some of those people—family, friends, co-workers. Some of them will have never heard of you, but it won't make what you leave them any less valuable.

Sometimes, you'll get to witness the fruits of your legacy. Sometimes, you'll have moved on. Either way, it matters to those who follow you.

Ask one extra, high-impact question when you're setting goals.

You may set goals quarterly or at the end of the year or all year long. Often, those goals are fairly "me" focused, e.g., "What do I want to create? How do I want to live?"

Next time, what if you were to play the long game and ask yourself one extra question: *What am I leaving behind for the people who follow me?*

For example:

- How can you set your current team up to thrive after you leave for a new role?

- What will your kids take with them after they move out of the home?

- What knowledge can you share now that people will access in the future?

- What are your encouraging words that will live on in someone's heart?

- How are you living and leading so that someone can model you years later?

I'm certain my dad wasn't thinking about legacy when he hid that key. But he did want someone else to benefit from his actions.

What about the people who will follow you?

● SECTION III:

YOUR FUEL: FEELING ALIVE AND STAYING INSPIRED

When you start any quest toward a big goal, you first get to experience the rush of dreaming big. Later, when you've achieved your goal, you experience the thrill and satisfaction of living your dream. In these moments, you feel truly alive.

Yet, most of life is lived somewhere in between those high points at the beginning and end—in the day-to-day of the mundane and the messy. If your dream is big, getting there is rarely easy or fast. In other words, you get even more of the mundane and the messy.

If we are only inspired and feel alive at the beginning or end of that quest, life can be long, lifeless, and frustrating. What fun is that?

What would it be like to feel alive and stay inspired every day, even if you're still far from achieving your biggest dreams? You free more of your genius when you're able to feel alive and inspired, even when things are difficult.

Here's the important myth to lay to rest: Many people believe that they fuel their success by never feeling satisfied, pushing themselves

● go to www.davidmartinco.com/ftg-videos

mercilessly, gritting their teeth at every step. They have a distaste for everything except for the achievement of their goals. They consider their never-satisfied attitude their secret success strategy.

But what if they're wrong? What if that's the "squelch the genius" approach? Just because many overachievers employ the never-satisfied strategy doesn't mean it's the most effective method.

Grinding on a goal and never being satisfied may work in the short term, but it produces diminishing returns. And it often creates unintended consequences of chronic stress symptoms, bad behaviors, and damaged relationships with key people. Does that sound like genius?

If you're in this for the long haul, you'll want to find satisfaction in the pursuit, not just at the end—even if doing so is difficult.

Relying heavily on dissatisfaction with where you are is like burning dirty fuel. You can reach your destination, perhaps. But you'll waste a lot of energy, and you'll stink up the place in the process.

Training yourself to feel alive and inspired even when things are not going as planned gives you clean fuel when others are sputtering.

In my experience with thousands of clients, finding ways to feel more alive and inspired NOW, even if you haven't yet landed your dream, isn't just a Pollyanna feel-good strategy. It reduces your own self-imposed friction, the unnecessary grinding that's slowing you down from achieving what you really dream of. Burning clean fuel makes you more successful, not less.

The chapters in this section share examples of people who've used this approach to access more of their strength. Each one offers you a different pathway to choose inspiration, no matter how difficult your current stage of the journey is.

17

DO YOU HAVE THE GUTS TO RISK IT ALL LIKE SHE DOES?

To feel fully alive, you can't squelch yourself.

Not long ago, my wife, Brenda, and I saw a fantastic cabaret show. Everyone on the stage played full-out.

The star was Jane Lynch.

But truthfully, we were mostly there to see my wife Brenda's long-time friend, Kate Flannery, who was also in the show. You might know Kate as Meredith from *The Office*. (Yes, she's as fun in person as she is on TV.)

One element from this show biz stage translates 100% to your leadership stage. If you can pull this off, you'll *never* lack a loyal following, because fully engaged leaders draw a crowd.

Pros know their jobs and play their parts.

Kate's played many roles in her 30+ years in show business. In this show, she was singing with and providing on-stage hilarity for her friend Jane, along with a great crooner, Tim Davis. They were backed up by the super-hot Tony Guerrero Quintet. It was a team of eight real pros playing their parts.

Jane's gift is dead-pan and steady humor, so Kate's role in this show is to be quick and over-the-top outrageous. Kate delivered perfect harmonies while throwing her body around the stage, getting people to laugh so hard they cried—even during sad folk songs. The contrast made Jane even more entertaining.

Kate got the entire audience to engage; everyone was clapping or waving their arms at inappropriate times. If they didn't, she called them out in a fun way until they joined in. Even the band musically zigged instead of zagging to keep the audience alive.

The audience never knew what was going to happen, so we had to pay attention.

These pros know a stage secret:

We are craving someone who will dare to fail right in front of us. We're more awake and alive because they're willing to risk it all as we watch.

Being fully exposed is fully rewarded.

We're drawn to someone who will take the risk and perform without a net. We don't feel nearly as connected to the neatly scripted and expertly edited performance.

So much is staged and scripted in the world that we bond with a person willing to risk it all with us.

- The Grateful Dead created ravenously loyal fans by making it up every night, not by making edited albums in the studio.

- Poorly shot YouTube videos of real-life events get more views than the cleaner, voiced-over versions on the ten o'clock news.

- Millions tune in for *So You Think You Can Dance* and *The Voice* to watch people willing to risk public failure to pursue their dreams.

Your audience wants you to give them two things—this applies to leaders, not just performers.

- The unpredictable/surprise: This keeps us alert and helps us feel more alive.

- Participation/co-creation: This helps us feel that we've contributed, and it reminds us that we matter.

Unskilled "winging it" doesn't work.

Jane Lynch's cabaret act wasn't just a bunch of hacks cutting up on stage. All eight performers honed their skills for years. Plus, they rehearsed this show tirelessly before they hit the road.

On that foundation, they could cut loose live on stage and invite the audience to be a part of the show.

You can do the same: Train and rehearse ad nauseam. Then, be real.

How much are you willing to risk for loyalty and engagement?

- Do you deliver the fully scripted presentation, or do you invite unpredictable dialogue?
- Do you allow true Q&A at town halls, or do you plant friendly questions in the audience?
- Do you conveniently forget to include dissenters in decision-making, or do you take the risk to build something even better?

The opportunity to co-create with you gets people to invest unreasonably.

We drove two hours each way to catch this show and didn't get to bed until 2:30 the next morning. I'd have done it again the next day if I could have.

The people you want to inspire feel the same way.

Are you inviting them to join you in a live performance or to observe your squeaky-clean delivery of the company line?

If you're asking me to bring my all, show me *you're* all in.

18

LEGALIZED MIND CONTROL: WHY PEOPLE CAN'T LOOK AWAY FROM YOU

For 10, 15, and 20 years, elite athletes will prepare to win gold in the Olympics. But for much longer, TV network executives have been preparing in a different way to guarantee you'll stay tuned in more than you'd planned to.

Their secret is 100% relevant if *you* want to win gold in the areas that matter to you.

How do the TV networks keep you coming back?

It's hidden in plain sight: storytelling.

A well-told story will inspire you to act in ways that defy logic—including staying glued to the screen when it's past time for bed. It's legalized mind control. You can't look away.

If it was just athletes racing on a track or swimming laps in a pool with no stories, it might catch your eye. But you wouldn't rearrange your life to keep tuning in.

It's the stories.

National pride stories. Personal dream stories. Underdog stories. They're like a siren song.

Stories hook your brain and heart.

Stories hook the emotional and social parts of your brain, superseding logic and priorities. It keeps you magnetized to the screen long beyond your intention.

Network executives know you just can't resist the behind-the-scenes story about an underdog athlete or a team plagued by injury.

Add in the hook no one can resist: no guaranteed victories.

The Olympics aren't an action movie where your hero always wins. Olympic drama is real, and your hero could lose.

Will Michael Phelps do it again? No guarantees. You have to keep watching to the end.

Stories change your actions—leverage it!

When stories hook us, they cause us to act in ways that defy logic and reasoning. Stories get us to blast through fears and obstacles. Without stories, you'd never do anything great.

You don't need steroids to fly high. You need an awesome story.

A good story will win you gold.

Let these three levels of story "Olympicize" your success so you can't look away from your own dreams.

LEVEL ONE: THE HERO'S STORY IS YOUR STORY

Story experts note that we listen to stories autobiographically. A story of an Olympian who struggled through overwhelming difficulties makes you think of your own struggles. Their grit to persevere reminds you of your own grit.

Be shameless. Let these athletes' stories remind you of your own awesomeness.

LEVEL TWO: OLYMPIANS TELL OLYMPIC-SIZED STORIES

The most important story for an elite athlete is the one she tells *to herself about herself*. What kind of a story do you think they're telling?

Unless her stories of herself were as big as her dreams, she'd never have endured the years of grueling training to arrive at the Olympics.

A story alone will not make anyone an Olympian. But if her story isn't big enough, she need not bother. Our autobiography predicts our future.

LEVEL YOU: HOW GRAND IS YOUR AUTOBIOGRAPHY?

What's the story you're telling about yourself? Really, answer that question for your own sake. Your answer determines your future. It will either give you fuel or drain your fuel. You'll most need this fuel when things are falling apart all around you and the stress is overbearing. And even if you never speak it out loud, when you tell yourself the story that makes you more powerful, you live differently. As you do so, people can't resist wanting to watch you. You're living a real story right in front of them.

Just like athletes, your level of success and satisfaction won't exceed the level of your autobiography. But a well-told story can fuel your drive to gold.

How big is your story? Is it as inspiring as your dreams?

19

BRUCE SPRINGSTEEN DISPENSES HUMAN ROCKET FUEL IN 6 WORDS

Springsteen took me to inspiration school.

Oh, yeah. He can sing too.

The Boss got right down to it.

Put yourself there… a huge stadium is bulging with tens of thousands of people. The buzz of excited conversations fills the air.

Suddenly, the lights across the arena drop to black, and the conversations stop. You can hear some people start to clap and whistle.

You can't see him, but The Boss walks onto the stage and up to the mic.

In the darkness, you hear his twangy, raspy voice booming out of the mega speakers as he howls, "Is there anybody *alive* out there?!" The crowd comes to its feet.

Again, "Is there anybody *alive* out there?!" The crowd screams and claps louder.

He shouts those six words four or five times until every person in the crowd is screaming their lungs out.

When the energy in the stadium peaks, the stage lights flash up, and the band breaks into its first song. The band and the crowd never looked back. Everyone was fully alive.

Is there anybody *alive* out there?

Bruce cut to the chase for all of us. In the end, isn't that why you're doing whatever it is you do? Not just to stay alive but to be alive. To *feel* alive.

You pursue outrageous goals. You work hard. You engage with challenging people. You live your life large in many ways, ever in pursuit of that feeling of being fully alive.

So what's this got to do with living your dreams?

Steal like an artist. Or rather, steal *from* an artist.

Stop for a moment and picture all of the people you're leading. They want the same thing as you do: *to feel more alive.*

And many of them are looking to *you* to help them feel it. You're their leader, and they're ready to play bigger and be more alive.

No, it's not your responsibility to help them feel alive. But when you create opportunities for them to be a part of something bigger than themselves and stretch and learn, feeling more alive is the gift you give them. We gladly follow the people who help us feel alive.

And this vibrancy is the fuel that will keep everyone going even when the odds are impossible and the challenges keep growing.

No wonder everyone loves The Boss in concert (and Beyoncé and Bruno too).

The leaders who inspire us aren't just playing big for themselves. They're helping the people around them raise their game and feel more alive. And in the process, the gift comes back to them. They lay it all on the line for their people, fully alive, just like Bruce did that night.

What do your people want from you? They're saying, "Show me how I can come fully to life, and I'll follow you anywhere… and in the process, I'll deliver some magnificent results."

Your crowd is waiting. Step up to the mic.

20

ROCKY BALBOA SHOWS YOU HOW TO KEEP THE DREAM ALIVE

If your success waned, would you persevere for 40 years to get back to the top of your game? How about 20 years? Or even two?

How you answer those questions probably says more about the success of your dreams than any job-related skill you have.

Sylvester Stallone and Matt Damon gave a tutorial on how to keep the dream alive.

The Golden Globe Awards are a major recognition of accomplishment in film and television. It's super competitive because there is so much great talent… *just like at your work.*

Sylvester Stallone and Matt Damon both received mega-recognition for the first films of their careers, *Rocky* and *Good Will Hunting*, respectively. In 2016, they finally won again.

For Stallone, that was almost 40 years ago. For Damon, almost 20. The acceptance speeches for Stallone and Damon should be required viewing for anyone who has a dream so big it could take decades to fulfill.

It took a *long* time to make it back to the top.

While both have had plenty of success over the years, neither had been recognized again as *the best* with a Golden Globe until now.

In their acceptance speeches, both acknowledged how long it had been. Damon said, "…I've made a lot of movies that people just didn't go see…." But he kept making movies. And so did Stallone.

Would you be able to hang in there for that long?

Will you be recognized for your accomplishment in 2040? What about 2060? Let Stallone and Damon school you on what it takes.

They demonstrate two *skills* that allowed them to rise again decades after their last mega-successes:

1. resilience, and

2. courage

Resilience and courage are *skills* you build, not God-given talents.

Resilience: This is your ability to get back in the game at full power after failure and setback.

How strong is your resilience?

If you're doing something big, you're going to encounter countless obstacles and setbacks. How willing are you to keep bouncing back to achieve your goals? What if it took two years to succeed? 20 years? 40?

Count on setbacks. Your talent and skill are empty shells without the resilience to keep going when most people want to quit.

Resilience is a choice you can make every day, and each time you do, it becomes more a part of you.

Courage: Courage is borne from your connection to a bigger reason, something bigger than yourself. It could be a person, a cause, a group, an outcome. It keeps you going.

Courage is one of the few emotions strong enough to overcome fear. You'll never avoid feeling fear, so you'll need to constantly stoke your courage. How strong is your courage—your connection to something bigger than you are?

What or who do you care about deeply? That's where you'll find more courage.

Live where the air is rare.

Stallone and Damon are remarkable because few people would have remained as resilient and courageous as they did. Because of that, they breathe rarified air.

The same is true among your colleagues. Few will develop the resilience and courage to do all they're capable of. But you can if you understand what it takes and build it.

What would it mean for you to commit to your dreams like this?

21

ACTING LIKE A FIRST RESPONDER IN CRISIS

In the last several years, around the world, we've been reminded that we cannot go it alone. Hurricanes, fires, and floods have put many people in danger and have turned worlds upside down.

In these dire situations, many people step up to support each other. They make sacrifices and take risks often for total strangers they'll never see again.

During one crisis, 250 first responders from Nashville drove to Florida days before Hurricane Irma made landfall so they could be ready to jump into action. Until the professionals could respond, residents in every community improvised rescues to free their neighbors who were in danger.

The world can simultaneously be an incredibly threatening place *and* a kind and generous place.

Some people dedicate their lives to stepping up for others.

Some of the most praiseworthy people on the planet are first responders. They're courageous women and men who risk their own well-being to help total strangers when they're most vulnerable and in need.

How could you not respect these people?

They understand the huge risks of doing their job, and they choose to do it anyway. In fact, the greater the peril for the people they're helping, the more risk they seem to be willing to face.

Here's the part that doesn't add up.

As a way of keeping us safe and alive, human brains are wired to feel fear when we perceive danger. Fear gives us three clear choices: fight, flight, and freeze.

However, walking into danger to help someone else, especially someone you don't even know, is *not* on that list.

What makes a first responder go against their natural fear and put themselves at risk?

Thankfully, there are forces in all of us even stronger than fear. One of them is courage—the emotion you feel when you're dedicating yourself to something bigger than you.

First responders absolutely feel fear. But they're so dedicated to the bigger cause of serving and caring for others, they generate a courage even more powerful than fear.

In a catastrophe like a hurricane, there aren't enough first responders.

Suddenly, ordinary citizens start to take risks and make sacrifices to support others. Especially in extreme conditions, any one of us can recognize a cause or purpose bigger than ourselves is at play.

Courage is always there within us. And when it's evoked, ordinary people do extraordinary things.

The personal benefits of courage.

While no one does it for this reason, acting with courage on behalf of another generates an increased sense of meaning within yourself.

When you're overwhelmed by deadlines and schedules and frustrations, life might not feel so meaningful. But in that moment when you step up for someone else, you realize you matter greatly.

What if…

What if we could align ourselves just a wee bit more with the causes and purposes we know are bigger than us?

The fear will still show up.

The fear our brains generate every day can be strong. Courage can be stronger.

The point is, courage is always there.

We all understand this. When asked, "What would you do if you had 10 times the courage you have now?" most people can answer quickly what they would do.

In other words, you probably already know what matters so much to you that it would help you generate greater courage. Put your attention there.

The people stepping up to help total strangers remind us of the courage that exists in every human. *Every human.*

It goes deeper.

I believe there is something that lies beneath courage that's fueling it all. Pardon my French, but it's love. The real generator driving courage is love. When you dedicate yourself to something bigger than you, isn't that really what you're feeling?

The overwhelm and fear we feel when we focus on deadlines and burdens can dampen anyone's spirit.

What would *you* do if you had 10 times the courage you have now?

The part of you that answers is the first responder in you. Take a step in that direction now.

You don't need a hurricane to remind you.

22

DO YOU GIVE DIVORCE GIFTS? YOU'LL NEED WHAT MY FRIEND GAVE ME

I'm re-gifting a valuable gift from a friend.

When I went through a divorce many years ago, I fought hard to avoid the chaos and public humiliation I was anticipating. I just wanted to withdraw from the world.

I felt like a pathetic failure.

I holed myself up in my friend Virgil's apartment in Chicago, hoping the world wouldn't notice if I just disappeared. I'm sure I looked pretty foolish trying to hide and hold everything together rather than move toward my next phase of life.

Perhaps you've tried this move once or twice yourself? If you've ever fallen on your face publicly, you know what I'm talking about.

Essentially, I was fighting change.

If you are resisting change or living through a tough transition, this applies to you too.

Then, one morning, a gracious gift appeared in my inbox.

A friend who noticed I was avoiding the inevitable thoughtfully emailed me a short essay/poem to read. Everything changed after reading it. Someday, or maybe today, you're going to need it too.

In the years since then, I've dusted this off for hundreds of clients who were experiencing their own tough transitions. They always thank me. Every time I share it, I use that as an excuse to re-read it.

Take a minute to enjoy this piece of poetic profundity right now. It's a brief but valuable read—worth reading now and saving to re-read to fuel you through every tough transition.

Sadly, the author is no longer living, but he was a wise man.

The Parable of the Trapeze*

Turning the Fear of Transformation into the Transformation of Fear

by Danaan Parry

Sometimes I feel that my life is a series of trapeze swings. I'm either hanging on to a trapeze bar swinging along or, for a few moments in my life, I'm hurtling across space in between trapeze bars.

Most of the time, I spend my life hanging on for dear life to my trapeze-bar-of-the-moment. It carries me along at a certain steady rate of swing and I have the feeling that I'm in control of my life.

I know most of the right questions and even some of the answers.

But every once in a while as I'm merrily (or even not-so-merrily) swinging along, I look out ahead of me into the distance, and what do I see? I see another trapeze bar swinging toward me. It's empty and I know, in that place in me that knows, that this new trapeze bar has my name on it. It is my next step, my growth, my aliveness coming to get me. In my heart of hearts I know that, for me to grow, I must release my grip on this present, well-known bar and move to the new one.

---

* *The Parable of the Trapeze* is taken from the book *Warriors of the Heart* by Danaan Parry and used with permission. The book may be purchased at the Earthstewards Network website, www.earthstewards.org.
Please do not use without specific permission from the Earthstewards Network. To discuss permission, contact publishing@earthstewards.org.

Each time it happens to me I hope (no, I pray) that I won't have to let go of my old bar completely before I grab the new one. But in my knowing place, I know that I must totally release my grasp on my old bar and, for some moment in time, I must hurtle across space before I can grab onto the new bar.

Each time, I am filled with terror. It doesn't matter that in all my previous hurtles across the void of unknowing I have always made it. I am each time afraid that I will miss, that I will be crushed on unseen rocks in the bottomless chasm between bars. I do it anyway. Perhaps this is the essence of what the mystics call the faith experience. No guarantees, no net, no insurance policy, but you do it anyway because somehow to keep hanging on to that old bar is no longer on the list of alternatives. So, for an eternity that can last a microsecond or a thousand lifetimes, I soar across the dark void of "the past is gone, the future is not yet here."

It's called "transition." I have come to believe that this transition is the only place that real change occurs. I mean real change, not the pseudo-change that only lasts until the next time my old buttons get punched.

I have noticed that, in our culture, this transition zone is looked upon as a "no-thing," a noplace between places. Sure, the old trapeze bar was real, and that new one coming toward me, I hope that's real, too. But the void in between? Is that just a scary, confusing, disorienting nowhere that must be gotten through as fast and as unconsciously as possible?

NO! What a wasted opportunity that would be. I have a sneaking suspicion that the transition zone is the only real thing and the bars are illusions we dream up to avoid the void where the real change, the real growth, occurs for us. Whether or not my hunch is true, it remains that the transition zones in our lives are incredibly rich places. They should be honored, even savored. Yes, with all the pain and fear and feelings of being out of control that can (but not necessarily) accompany transitions, they are still the most alive, most growth-filled, passionate, expansive moments in our lives.

We cannot discover new oceans unless we have the courage to lose sight of the shore.

So, transformation of fear may have nothing to do with making fear go away, but rather with giving ourselves permission to "hang out" in the transition between trapezes. Transforming our need to grab that new bar, any bar, is allowing ourselves to dwell in the only place where change really happens. It can be terrifying. It can also be enlightening in the true sense of the word. Hurtling through the void, we just may learn how to fly.

23

WOULD YOU USE YOUR POWER LIKE THEY DID?

Back in 2003, a famous incident occurred in Major League Baseball. The baseball story is just the backdrop. The real story is about power—and how you'd use yours.

One fateful night.

On October 14, 2003, the Chicago Cubs had to win just one more game to do something they hadn't done since 1945: win the National League Pennant.

With one out in the eighth inning in a game against the Florida Marlins, the Cubs were winning 3-0.

Just five more outs would secure the historic win. Cubs fans around the world could taste 58 years of redemption.

The anticipation was palpable.

The next batter popped a foul ball into the first row of the stands in left field. As the ball fell into the stands, several fans lurched for the ball to try to collect a historic souvenir.

The fans were looking up at the ball.

They didn't notice that the Cubs' left fielder, Moisés Alou, was racing to the ball and leapt to catch it… just as one fan deflected it. No catch. Alou threw his glove to the ground and stomped his feet in anger.

Out of respect, let's call the fan who touched the ball "Dedicated Cubs Fan." That's what he was.

Whether Alou would have caught the ball remains a great debate. But after his missed catch, the Cubs gave up *eight* runs in that inning and lost the game, 8-3.

They played the Marlins again the next night, still needing to win just one game. They lost again.

The Marlins didn't win the pennant. The Cubs lost it.

As a lifelong Cubs fan, my heart sank like everyone else's. But was there another reason the Cubs didn't win?

True champions don't complain when they get a bad break. They get back in the game and find a way to win. To me, that was the real loss for the Cubs.

Here's where it gets insane: power used without thought.

Even though the Cubs had multiple opportunities to win that night and the next day, they didn't.

Yet, suddenly, thousands of loud and angry Cubs fans decided to blame the Dedicated Cubs Fan for not winning the pennant because he tipped one ball. He was threatened during the game and pelted with beers even as security eventually escorted him out of the stadium for his safety.

By the next morning, the Dedicated Cubs Fan's name and home address had been plastered across the internet. Chicago police posted squad cars outside his house as news trucks and angry fans surrounded his home.

Although the Dedicated Cubs Fan issued a heartfelt and sincere apology the next morning, the flames of misdirected anger had already lit up the decades-dry kindling of frustration.

Since 2003, this guy's name and face have been plastered across the internet. Commentators and fans won't let it die. Anger gets viewers, after all.

I'm not exaggerating when I say that a tipped ball changed every part of this guy's life since then.

Cubs Rule!

In 2016, the Chicago Cubs won the pennant *and* the World Series for the first time in 108 years.

Cubs fans around the world bowed at the feet of the World Champions who'd finally answered their prayers.

As the team who performed this epic feat, many people granted them extreme power and authority. At that moment, everything they did and said carried greater weight.

How'd they use their power?

A few months after the Cubs' great victory, they gave the Dedicated Cubs Fan his own 2016 World Series ring with his name engraved on it.

The owners and leaders of the Cubs understood the power they had, and they decided to use it to support a fan who definitely deserved far better than he got.

Quietly, the Dedicated Cubs Fan received the ring and issued a statement through his attorney expressing extreme gratitude—and asking to be left alone.

Let's hope that this act of power creates a bit more sanity in this guy's life.

Here's the bigger question: What would you do?

What if you had extreme power to exercise? What if you had the attention of people who respect you, if your words and actions carried extraordinary weight?

Would you leverage your power to:

- make an endorsement or introduction to help smooth a deserving person's path?

- step up to support a great person who'd just caught a bad break?

- show interest in a struggling project you thought had merit?

- just be a decent person to someone who could use extra kindness today?

Who's done that for you when you needed it?

You can just as easily use your power to tear people down for lunging for a ball—or some other small thing. That's your call.

Here's the secret.

You may not have just won the World Series, but you *do* have that power right now.

How are you going to use it?

● SECTION IV:

YOUR IDENTITY: ON A MISSION:
A CHAMPION FOR A CAUSE
(AKA, AN UNDERDOG)

If you are building something that matters deeply to you, you're probably thinking about it even when you're not working on it. You're imagining how it could make an even greater difference. You're obsessing about how to get there faster or how you could do it better.

Simply put, you're on a mission.

Being on a mission usually means you're pursuing something that's much greater than you are, perhaps something you've never tried before. Maybe it's even something no one has ever done before.

Yet, there's a complication. Or maybe it's really good news.

The moment you decide to pursue something you just can't NOT pursue, you've likely placed yourself in a situation where the odds are stacked against your success. If it were easy, you wouldn't be quite so inspired by it. Plus, someone else would've probably already done it.

● go to www.davidmartinco.com/ftg-videos

Here's the important thing to know: When you sign up for a big mission, you place yourself into an elite, underrated category: the underdog.

The odds are stacked against an underdog. The odds are stacked against you.

Look at the people you've come to respect. While they may be flying high today, at some point, they were almost certainly sitting in the underdog position. They experienced extreme setbacks and ran into too many dead ends to count. Yet, they cared so much about their bigger goal that they continued. The failure and challenge strangely brought out more of their best.

In the process of pursuing a goal that was so ridiculously out of reach, the once-dormant seeds of genius sprang up like they never would have had all of the odds been in their favor.

This section helps you connect with that part of you who's a person on a mission, filled with an underdog spirit that relentlessly calls out the best in you.

Few people would willingly sign up for the underdog role—until they understand what a powerful position it is to be in. Keep dreaming, even if everyone tells you it can't happen. At the very least, you'll access strength you haven't experienced before. You'll likely surprise many people (mostly yourself) with what you're capable of.

24

THE CLASSIC UNDERDOG STORY
YOU'LL LIVE MANY TIMES
(IF YOU'RE LUCKY)

Fortified by failure.

I recently had lunch with Jeff, my best friend from high school.

Today, Jeff's an über-successful insurance agent. I see his face plastered on a giant roadside billboard ad every time I drive back to Illinois to visit my parents, and it always makes me smile.

But Jeff wasn't always at the top.

I don't know how we landed on the topic, but over fish tacos, we talked about some of our heartbreaking defeats in life. You've had a few, right?

Jeff could run like the wind.

His sophomore year of high school, Jeff's two-mile relay team took first at the Illinois State Track Meet. It was an epic come-from-behind victory, still one of the most exciting sporting events I've witnessed—and a really big deal in our little hometown.

The next year, Jeff "The State Champion" returned with a swagger to the State Track Meet with the fastest qualifying time in the state in the half-mile run. He called his dad the night before and said, "I'm gonna win this."

But he didn't. In fact, he finished twelfth out of 12 runners in the finals in front of a crowd of 10,000.

Heartbreak of teenage proportions.

Jeff was embarrassed and unhappy in only a way that a teenager can be. Crushed. Devastated. Cooler heads told him to just be happy he'd made it to State.

But Jeff wasn't happy. However, he *was* smart… because he let his teenage heartbreak fuel a turnaround, rethinking everything and rewriting his approach.

Jeff's story is the classic underdog story.

If you want to challenge or disrupt your world, you're going to get knocked down many times. It doesn't matter how successful you've been in the past. When you make a big stretch, you are going to fail miserably. Many people interpret this as failure and give up.

However, true challengers lick their wounds, take the lessons away from it, and start again with a stronger and wiser perspective.

Overcoming success.

In that moment, the hardest and most important move to make is "overcoming success." It's when you recognize that your past success strategies that helped you get to this point are now the very things that stand in the way of your future success. The more success you've had with those strategies, the harder it is to release them and develop new ones.

That's the essence of overcoming success. Jeff's work was "overcoming success," and he did it.

One year later, Jeff won the State Track Meet in the two-mile run and took fifth in the one-mile. Earlier in the fall, he also placed second in the State Cross Country Meet. His times are still among the best in Illinois history.

Jeff admits that none of this would have happened without his heartbreak the year before.

Show me a meaningful accomplishment you fought hard to achieve, and I can show you a heartbreaking failure that preceded it. It's the classic story of the underdog—fortified by failure.

Good news! Heartbreak signals a loss of all hope.

When you feel heartbroken, it's because you know it's over without question. It's a total loss. No repair is possible. All hope is lost, and that's the best possible news for you.

When a client of mine reaches that place, I know they're on the verge of a breakthrough if they can understand what's really happening, withstand the emotional pain (embarrassment, despair, sadness, anger), and get back up for the next round.

Surrender is great news!!!

When you're completely devastated and ready to give up, you're willing to question your deepest assumptions, beliefs, motives, and goals. What a great opening! Only when you're feeling hopeless will you be open to possibly finding a different view and a new approach. As long as there's a sliver of hope left in you, you'll keep hanging on to your old ways that no longer serve you.

In that moment of heartbreak, you'll feel despair. You'll have no solutions. You've finally reached beyond the limits of your knowledge and skill. All is lost. You surrender… at least, for now.

When you recognize that everything you know is inadequate for you in this situation, that is when you open yourself to new, revolutionary insights and solutions you'd have never considered if your old approach was still working.

Most people want to avoid that feeling of absolute anguish that temporarily overcomes them, so they retreat back to their old ways, defending them and trying to hold them together with Band-Aids and baling wire rather than letting them go.

When they do that, they miss the miraculous insights that exist on the other side of acknowledging that their current thinking is failing them. The risk of letting go of what you've believed in feels too scary. Most people stay put and keep fighting for their old success strategies.

This is why viewing yourself as an underdog can be an advantage. It's why underdogs so often come out of nowhere to surprise us. With the mindset of an underdog, you realize you have nothing to lose anyway. So, you don't fight to hold onto your current approach. You let go of what you've tried, and you open yourself up to new insights.

This is exactly what Jeff did. He gave up on his old approach that had failed him and opened up to new approaches, which would have seemed radical or ridiculous through the lens of his old reality.

Heartbreak is the true breakfast of champions.

If you really want to revolutionize your world, heartbreaks will be a regular part of your diet. While heartbreak may not feel like good news as it's happening, it's the turning point in the underdog journey. It changes everything.

What's breaking your heart right now?

Did someone betray you? Did your new business fall apart? Did you get your ass kicked in public?

Do not squander this heartbreak! Who knows when the next opportunity to paint a new, powerful worldview and action plan may come? Heartbreak and confusion lie at the threshold of breakthroughs.

Jeff's Epilogue: In December of the year Jeff and I had lunch, his insurance agency finished fifth in the company standings in Illinois. On the drive home from the awards banquet, he told his wife, "We can do better." He's learned to never squander the opportunity of a good defeat.

Wanna guess how things ended for his business that year?

25

IT'S PREDICTABLE: YOU'RE GOING TO THINK YOU'RE CRAZY

Mel asked me to meet him for a drink at an out-of-the-way dive bar. He wanted to talk away from the office where people wouldn't overhear us.

After a quick hello, he jumped right into why he wanted to talk.

"Can I ask you a question?"

"Sure. What's up?"

"Do you think I'm losing it? I'm beginning to think I must be crazy."

He wasn't speaking metaphorically. I could tell from his demeanor that Mel sincerely believed something was wrong with him.

Freeze that frame for a moment.

If someone asked to meet you at a remote location and, 60 seconds into the conversation, he told you he might be losing it… *How would you have responded?*

I did not call a doctor.

Luckily, I've met a thousand "Mels" over the years, and I was pretty certain he was right on schedule.

You might be Mel someday. Really.

If you're a person who often challenges and disrupts the system because you see that something much better is possible, you may someday have a "Mel Moment" too.

He was living out a classic scenario.

Here it is, step-by-step:

1. Mel's new company, "Acme," had been prosperous for years.

2. Recently, some upstart competitors started eating Acme's lunch. (Those competitors were playing like underdogs, by the way. That's why they were having success. As Jeff's story taught in the previous chapter, you know what an advantage an underdog mindset can be.)

3. Acme asked first one and then another internal leader to take Acme back to the top. Back to back, they failed. They left the company "to pursue other interests." (Why did they fail? Because they simply doubled down on the outdated approaches that had worked for years. They couldn't surrender and acknowledge the old ways were failing them.)

4. Acme hired an outsider, Mel, to catch them up to current times. (They were hoping he'd bring a fresh new point of view to the problem… but there were seeds of problems planted in this. Acme hadn't fully acknowledged how much their past success strategies were part of today's problem. They said they were all in but were mostly hoping for a Band-Aid, not a full surrender. Overcoming success is extremely difficult when you've been at the top.)

Save us!

When Mel was hired, he had an impassioned mandate from the President: Take us back to the top!

Mel brought fresh outsider eyes and years of experience. He quickly uncovered what was wrong and what good was possible. He enthusiastically started to paint the picture of a much better future.

Heads nodded. People applauded.

Yet, behind closed doors, when people had him alone, they said things like:

"There is no problem. We've just had a few soft years."

"That won't work. We've tried it before."

"You are going to give away the store, and I will stop you."

But wait a second. *You* recruited *me*!"

People were initially rah-rah about the transformation Mel would lead. But when he started to do what he was hired to do, he met everything from denial to active resistance.

No wonder he thought he was losing it.

People had a variety of reasons, but they agreed on one thing: it was *his* opinions that they universally opposed. What people *said they wanted* and how they were *actually acting* were completely incongruent. (Remember those seeds of problems that had been planted?)

Mel started asking, "Am I trapped in an alternate universe?"

Nothing was what he thought it was. This cognitive dissonance of being told by everyone they wanted to change while those same people actively resisted it could shake any person to the core.

After a few months of being able to make no sense of reality, he reached the only remaining conclusion: "There's something wrong with *me*. I'm the common denominator here. *I'm* the one who's crazy."

As predictable as sunrise—for you, too.

The people you're leading to the promised land *that they'll insist they want to get to* will predictably contradict themselves, and here's why:

People are enthusiastic for the *outcome* of the change.

Of course! We all want nirvana!

They just don't want to live through the *process* of the change.

"Are you kidding? It threatens my reality, my power, my identity. That's messy and uncomfortable. No thank you!" Essentially, they're still attached to their old success strategies. It's not just an intellectual attachment. It's deeply emotional.

If you forget this, you may someday think you're losing it too. However, you don't have to, and neither did Mel.

Mel bounced back.

He got clear that this wasn't a personal problem. It was a leadership challenge.

He developed an influencing strategy to help people *act* in congruence with the outcomes they said they wanted. It took three years and counting, and it was painful for many people until they started to see successes in the new strategies. Still, Acme has reinvented itself internally and in the market.

The moral of the story.

When you are challenging and disrupting the system you're a part of, you will face resistance. Don't confuse predictable resistance with your personal sanity, although it's easy to do.

If you can overcome this first big obstacle, you've slain one of your biggest dragons: your own self-doubt.

Believing you might be crazy is a part of the challenger's journey. But it doesn't have to be the final stop.

26

HE WINS CHAMPIONSHIPS BY PICKING LOSERS

The Chicago Cubs' amazing success in 2016 after 108 years of failure is a story that relates to you more than it might seem. What can you gain from applying the story to your own life? More wins and a larger fan base.

But it might appear too risky. You decide.

The Cubs hadn't won a World Series since 1908. In 2016, they won it all.

Full disclosure: I'm a lifelong Cubs fan, but this chapter is written for you even if you don't like the Cubs or baseball.

The Cubs had surged.

In the few years before the championship, the Cubs became a new team. However, it's what happened long before any of these players were famous that makes them champions. It's the unattractive stuff no one likes to talk about.

But first, what's happening behind the curtain?

The Cubs players and Coach Joe Maddon won the games on the field. But the wizard behind the scenes is Theo Epstein, their President of Baseball Operations. One of his critical roles is finding the greatest talent for Coach Maddon to work with.

He's *really* good at finding talent.

Before he joined the Cubs, Epstein helped rebuild the Boston Red Sox. They hadn't won a World Series since 1918, but the teams Epstein built won in 2004, 2007, and 2013.

Hmmm... Maybe this guy is worth paying attention to.

He looks at talent with a different eye.

Epstein considers the important sabermetrics (popularized in the book/movie *Moneyball*) for each player. But he lives by a different motto that's been summarized as "scouting the person more than the player."

In particular, Epstein wants to know what adversity the players have faced and how they overcame it—on and off the field.

Here's the sobering reality of life.

Everybody is going to lose big sometimes. But who among us has built the muscle of resilience to come back after they just got thrown to the pavement?

Others might have been surprised by the outcome of the National League Division Series game on October 11, but the players were not. The Cubs surged to overcome a three-run deficit in the final inning to defeat the Giants. Ridiculous!

It's the biggest comeback in a final postseason game in Major League history. *That's* overcoming adversity, and every player on the field is an expert in it because of their ugly struggles of the past.

Epstein wants players who've faced adversity for a reason.

In fact, the team draws on their familiarity with past defeat for strength. After every game, the whole team would shout: "We never quit! We never quit!" almost like it's a cheer.

They're reinforcing their resilience muscles for the moments when they need them, like that Tuesday-night playoff game.

So, what's the lesson for you?

Just like world-class athletes, the adversity *you* overcame early in life really does make you stronger today.

But it's this messy past that most leaders want to sweep under the rug and hide from the rest of the world. Yet, as Epstein so wisely figured out, it's those who've lost and recovered who are most likely to win under pressure.

This messiness even makes people more loyal to them.

We love scruffy mutts even more because they've failed big—just like you and I have. We can see ourselves in their imperfection.

Don't fear the faux risk.

Many leaders believe their failures and missteps make them look unattractive. Failures are too risky to share. So they bury them and present their perfect image instead.

You know what we call the leaders who do that?

Boring. Unrelatable. Inauthentic. Untrustworthy.

Who wants to talk about how they lost?

You probably don't. But the huge screw-ups you overcame didn't just make you stronger. Being honest enough to talk about them openly (and wisely) also makes you a leader who people can connect with, someone they want to follow.

So, what's the stuff in your history that you wish no one knew about you? How did you crash and burn? How did you publicly embarrass yourself? And how are you stronger and wiser because of it?

Tell me about that, and I'll follow you anywhere.

27

HOW TO MANUFACTURE GOOD LUCK

You thought you were having a bad day?

What's your worst day look like? You're three months behind on your most important project with only one month until the deadline? You just caused a five-car pileup and found out you let your insurance policy lapse by a day?

You might even feel like you're cursed.

How about this for being cursed?

From the beginning of the 2016 baseball season, the Chicago Cubs were favored to win the World Series, the toughest competitive arena in baseball. After years of preparation and over six months of daily work to get here, they found themselves one game away from losing all they'd worked for—like so many times before. On a Saturday night in October, they were down three games to one in the World Series.

Only six teams in the 113-year history of the World Series had ever come back to win it all after being down three games to one. It'd been 31 years since the last team did it.

To make things worse, they would have to win the last two games on the road in front of a packed stadium of screaming Cleveland Indians fans.

We never quit.

Somehow, the Cubs scrapped back to win two straight games and catch up to Cleveland at three games to three.

We never quit.

Then, in the deciding game of the series, the Cubs leapt out to a 5-1 lead.

Cubs fans wanted to start celebrating. But 108 years of history—and the dreaded Curse of the Billy Goat—suggested they'd better keep cheering for their team through the last out.

Then, things went terribly wrong. *The curse was real!*

In a turnaround that took less than 90 seconds, Cleveland rallied back to tie the game at 6-6 in the next-to-last inning. They did this by scoring three runs off the Cubs' ace pitcher, who was supposed to be impossible to hit. It must be a curse.

The game was tied and headed into extra innings. The momentum was all Cleveland's. Hopeless, right?

After being so close to winning it all, Cubs fans were on the verge of once again shouting, "Wait until next year!" for the 109th consecutive winter.

We never quit.

It started to rain in Cleveland, and the umpires called a rain delay. During that 17-minute delay, the Cubs waited things out in the weight room beneath the stadium.

An unlikely leader stepped forward.

Jason Heyward, the Cubs' right fielder who'd only gotten three hits in seven games of the World Series, gathered the team to remind them of how they'd approached the entire season: WE NEVER QUIT!!!

If anyone had the right to feel cursed at that moment, it was this guy. In spite of his recent results at the plate, the mantra the Cubs had shouted all year was deep in his bones, and he became the unexpected voice for it.

When the game resumed, the Cubs immediately scored two runs. Ten minutes later, the Cubs were the 2016 World Champions.

We never quit.

Fans love baseball because it's like life.

The two teams in the World Series were incredibly talented. Talent was not the deciding factor in this World Series, though. It was living the simple motto that had become the Cubs' ethos: *"We never quit."*

Talent is the entry card to get you *into* your biggest game, whatever that is for you. But talent is abundant in this world, and it guarantees you nothing.

What gets you over the finish line rhymes with "never quit." It's called *grit*.

Grit is an invisible muscle you build.

It's not bestowed by genetics or privilege. In fact, the best way to build the muscle of *grit* is to get knocked down and get back up. Epic, frequent failure is your ally if you want to build your *grit* muscle.

Here's the punchline about *grit*: When "we never quit" lives deep in your bones, your motto might as well be "We manufacture good luck!" Rather, that's what it looks like when we watch the performance of people who've built up massive *grit*.

Grit makes you luckier. Or at least it appears that way, because it allows you to bounce back from challenges when most people had given up on you. Others can't "see" the grit you've developed since it's a personal quality within you. Therefore, the only plausible explanation they have for your success is: You got lucky.

Feeling cursed today?

Growing your *grit* muscle is anything but easy. But even the evil Curse of the Billy Goat can't stand up to the good luck that *grit* manufactures.

For those inevitable bad days that are headed your team's way at some unwelcome moment, you can start growing your *grit* today. You'll find yourself on the right side of luck.

May I suggest a mantra? *WE NEVER QUIT!*

28

SIX THINGS THAT HELP UNDERDOGS OVERCOME THE ODDS

Abraham Lincoln was born over 200 years ago. If there ever was an underdog you can learn from, it's him.

Heroes we celebrate today were almost always underestimated for large stretches of their lives. Because they challenged convention in such significant ways, the odds really were stacked against them.

They were underdogs.

This year, when people are predicting your failure because you're taking on a challenge that has wilted other people, remember the spirit of the underdog. Even the last three US presidents elected were laughable underdogs early in their campaigns.

Smart money would have never bet on Abraham Lincoln early in his career.

For all the reasons we've heard about in history class, Lincoln wasn't supposed to succeed. Yet, he was elected president and made some of the most bold, most controversial moves of any world leader in history.

Smart money would have never bet on Abraham Lincoln early in his presidency.

Before he even moved into the White House after his election, seven southern states had seceded from the Union. Even within his own hand-picked cabinet, he faced strong opposition, including one member who secretly lobbied for a presidential bid to challenge Lincoln in the next election.

Yet, while everyone else was still underestimating him as a country bumpkin, Lincoln birthed changes that altered the course of history not just in the US but around the world. He's the underdog's underdog.

That's because people predict future success or failure based on the external factors they can see (wealth, education, fame, size) and historical data they can point to (background, experience, past wins/losses). They're making the safe and reasonable bet.

But their analysis doesn't factor in the Arsenal of the Underdog.

Underdogs bet on their dreams.

They're not reckless. They bet on their dreams because they possess the Underdog's Arsenal, which "smart money" doesn't understand. How many of these six tools have you developed?

The Underdog's Arsenal includes tools like:

1) **New view:** A paradigm or point of view that challenges established wisdom and accepted traditions. You've mapped the territory differently, which allows you to navigate the same old terrain in a new way.

   Underdogs are rarely from within the mainstream group in power, so your view is undoubtedly different. This is your advantage. Your map looks like nonsense to the established power, but it will eventually become your advantage. It's this unique view that helps you understand that the impossible is actually possible. The people in power often think of it as foolish or reckless. Google was once a crazy idea. Bruce Springsteen and Elvis were kicked out of their first bands.

2) **Courage:** A desire to contribute to something much bigger than yourself, a driving force that won't let you quit.

Underdogs will face huge challenges that will evoke enormous amounts of fear. The odds are stacked against you, which is scary. Fear can be paralyzing. But underdogs have a hidden advantage: courage. Courage is an emotion that's stronger than fear, and you generate courage when you connect to a cause or purpose that's bigger than you are. Underdogs have a bigger cause. Courage prevails.

3) **Guidance:** You have a guide or confidant (think Yoda or Gandalf) who is showing you the map or helping you find unique ways to navigate it.

Almost every underdog has a wise guide whispering in their ear, helping to uncover and cultivate strength and wisdom that was hidden to them. The guide knows the territory and has no agenda except for your success. These tools are completely invisible to the outsider.

4) **Challenge mindset:** An attitude that views every event as a stepping stone or learning event, even when failure occurs.

Underdogs know obstacles and defeat better than most. They just view them differently—as challenges to learn from and overcome instead of as threats that could destroy them or their dreams. You're much more creative and resilient in the challenge mindset, which allows you to overcome obstacles most view as impassable.

5) **Sense of self:** You know who you are. You're not trying to be someone else or to please someone else. You identify yourself with the mission you're on.

Underdogs share the attitude that it's about the bigger mission, not about getting the credit. In fact, the more you can stay under the radar, the more success you often have. Without the worry of pleasing others, the burdens of doubt and distractions subside. You can just focus on how to keep things moving without so much self-critical talk.

6) **Practices and rituals:** You have activities that you repeat regularly to build skills and strength, usually when no one else is around.

Another invisible strength of the underdog is their practices. Because no one knows about your depth of practice, you are easier to underestimate. However, you know where you need to be stronger and wiser to succeed, so you practice to build those qualities in yourself constantly, even though no one else is. The strength you're building when the stress levels are low is what allows you to stay clear so you can soar when the pressure is so high that most people crumble.

If you don't have some of these six qualities now, today is a good day to start developing them.

Based on what is visible and measurable, the odds are against you.

But when you draw on your Arsenal, you'll find ways to keep going even though outsiders have written you off.

It's great to have examples of underdogs like Abraham Lincoln who remind us in a very public way that most great accomplishments started as laughable dreams. Your failure was predicted, though you still found your way.

Now, it's you who's reminding the rest of us that we can do big work too.

29

MARCH MADNESS CHAMPIONS: DO YOU SHARE THEIR KEY PREDICTOR OF SUCCESS?

March Madness descends upon us every year as winter starts to fade. Even if you don't like basketball, you can turn it into your own leadership development self-study program.

Don't you see a bit of yourself in those courageous athletes?

What's the best predictor of who will win?

The beauty of the men's and women's NCAA tournaments is that they're great equalizers. It doesn't matter what a team's win-loss record or national ranking was before the tournament.

If they qualify for the tournament, any one of them can be the champion. And talent is *not* the key differentiator.

We can predict one thing with certainty:

In every matchup, game plans will get blown apart. The competition will not behave as predicted. Refs will make bad calls.

The pressure will get to everyone at some moment.

Because of this, *resilience* is the key differentiator of who wins.

Resilience is measured by who can repeatedly get thrown off plan or knocked down *and* still return to their best game the most quickly and consistently.

This is where underdogs thrive. While everyone else was oohing and ahhing over the tallest and fastest, the underdogs have been quietly building their secret weapon: *resilience*.

Watch the games through this lens, and you'll see a whole new sport.

Who bounces back immediately instead of brooding over a bad pass? Who plays hard even when the coach picked someone else to take the last-second shot? Who instantly shakes off the terrible call by the ref?

In these nanoseconds of time, you'll watch champions being made. Rather, you'll watch those champions making themselves.

With a shortage of resilience, talent is diminished.

Because of the extreme pressure and stress of these games, every microgram of resilience matters. Every second faster you can bounce back affects the outcome. Talent is multiplied with resilience and reduced if it's lacking.

No one develops resilience overnight.

Resilience is built up day after day, year after year, disappointment after disappointment. It's a muscle.

It's no different for you.

It's not where you graduated from, where you worked before, or how many letters you have after your name. The key differentiator of your future success is your resilience.

How quickly do you bounce back after a big, public fail? Do you keep playing hard even when someone else got the promotion? Or what do you do when the budget for your biggest initiative gets cut?

Your life may seem very different than a college basketball game. But in some ways, it's the same: Obstacles, bad calls, and disappointments can materialize in an instant. And in that instant, you get to choose how quickly and how well you bounce back.

Resilience is your talent multiplier. Are you building the muscles of resilience?

30

THE INVISIBLE ADVANTAGE OF LEADERS ON A MISSION

On a Sunday morning in Manhattan, I had a seemingly ordinary brunch. I didn't think I was doing anything strange until I realized I was freaking out the bartender.

I was just trying to chill.

I'd just left a pretty intense training session. My teacher suggested I keep my mobile phone turned off to help integrate the learning. I did.

At the restaurant, I sat down at the bar on one of 20 or so empty barstools. The bartender chatted me up and took my order.

Then, he and the restaurant manager started hustling behind the bar to fill a large order of drinks for a big table of impatient guests.

I just watched.

With no phone to hold, I propped my elbows on the bar and looked around... at the displays of liquor on the shelves... at the industrial design features of the room... at the two people rushing to make the drinks.

I was the oddball.

After a few minutes, the manager walked up to me and said, "Sir, is everything ok? Do you need something? Have we not taken your order yet?"

I responded, "Yep, I'm good." She looked like she didn't believe me but got back to work.

Her questions made me wonder: Why did she think something was wrong?

Then, it hit me.

I was behaving extremely strangely. I was sitting at a bar with no one to talk to and no food to eat... and my face *wasn't* in my phone.

I was doing nothing—except being present.

When was the last time she'd seen a customer sit alone at her bar and just take everything in?

Clearly, something was wrong.

Why else would someone just sit there, by themselves, looking around the room?

Turning to our phones and other distractions is so common that a person stands out as odd if they're by themselves and *not* on their phone.

So I asked myself...

What's wrong with this picture? Study after study tells us that people long for authentic connections. We don't need scientists to tell us that's true!

Yet, in the moments when we could make a connection, we automatically turn to *packaged content* on a device for a dopamine hit instead of just being with the *real live content* in front of us.

Does this apply to you?

Is the stuff on the phone that awesome?

Or is it just easier than dealing with what's real—like being with the people or the place around us? Or heaven forbid, being with our own thoughts and feelings. Those are risky behaviors!

What is your go-to move?

Think back on your last several hours today. If you had a free moment, what did you do with it? If you were in a meeting, did you stay totally engaged? Were you present with the people who were talking to you? Did you glance at your phone?

It's easier to distract yourself than to be present.

The easy path is to focus on the packaged content on our phones rather than the real content in front of us. Crazy, right?

Here's why it matters:

- **Do you want to champion a revolution and change the world?**

  Without exception, the people who are changing their world have definitely mastered one invisible advantage: *They know how to manage their attention exceptionally well.* They've learned how to stay present far more often than taking the easier path of distraction, even under high stress. It's a skill I call having a *"mind to win."*

- **Can you change the world by yourself?**

  Or will you need help? The leaders who enroll others in their movement pay attention in a specific way. They stay present at an extreme level with the people who are helping them change the world. Having someone pay full attention to us is such a rare trait that it's a magnet that draws people to you. You know it for yourself. You've raised your game to support leaders who give you their full-on presence. They earn your loyalty.

- **You can have the best ideas in the world.**

  However, until you can stay relentlessly present with who and what is at hand, you squelch your power to deliver those ideas. Presence is the free, invisible superpower we rarely cultivate. Importantly, although people don't always know what it is, they do notice it—as I was reminded of on Sunday.

What do you care about so much that you're going to learn to bring your full presence to it?

● SECTION V:

YOUR SECRET WEAPON: THE WISDOM OF FRIENDING FAILURE*

The more success you've had, the more likely you'll stall when you fail. A person's successes positively reinforces their current thinking and approach. Even if what worked before stops working in the future, their previous success can become a sedative. As things start to fail, they're more likely to fall asleep at the wheel and keep steering in the same old direction.

With few failures in their past, they're less equipped to know how to respond when things stop working. As a result, they'll most likely view failure as their enemy, not their friend.

But here's what's predictable: If your dream is stretching you into new territory, you're going to fail frequently. Why is that? And what can you do about it?

When you name a goal that's big, important, and currently out of reach, your first move will likely be to apply your proven maps and methods in pursuit of this new goal. But your new goal stretches you into territory where many of your old solutions won't help you. You'll feel stuck,

● go to www.davidmartinco.com/ftg-videos

frustrated, confused. Most successful people will keep trying to use their old maps and success strategies long beyond their usefulness.

While it may not be obvious to you at that moment, feeling stuck and not knowing what to do is part of being the underdog. **It's an enviable position if you can make one critical move: befriend failure.**

The big challenges you face when you enter unknown territory will eventually tease out the best in you. But you must make failure your friend, not something you despise or avoid.

At this critical juncture, you get to choose your path forward. Will you double down on the thinking and approach that's always worked? Will you treat breakdowns as a threat and invest your energy in fighting to restore the old world where you knew how to win?

Or will you view the obstacle as a fun challenge to overcome? Will you ask what you're missing and what you don't know so you can create a learning agenda for success in the new world?

Every failure gives you an opportunity to recognize what you don't know and write a new success strategy. Going beyond those limits of what you know calls out your creative genius.

As soon as you lean into that process, your sense of meaning and contribution will grow. All because you befriended failure.

The chapters in this section share stories of people who had to figure out what to do when their old success strategies stopped working.

---

*   I know the correct words are "befriending failure," but I'm counting on the alliteration of "friending failure" to help this idea stick in your memory.

118

31

THE POWER MOVE FOR WHEN YOU'RE ABOUT TO FAIL OR QUIT

We live in a world that's always looking for the next hot idea. So when one idea lasts 75 years, there must be something to it.

Perhaps it could still guide you through your most difficult times for another 75 years?

This Power Move is hidden in an old movie that draws millions of viewers year after year.

Yes, the movie has a happy ending, but that's not why it remains popular.

People often overlook the timeless insight it carries because it doesn't seem that powerful. But once you've tried it for yourself, you'll know it's pure dynamite.

You can turn this insight into a habit to navigate your greatest challenges—while feeling happy and whole.

If you turn on your TV in December, you'll have many opportunities to view the movie *It's a Wonderful Life*. If you're not familiar with the story, here's a quick synopsis. Just skip it if you already know the story.

Story Synopsis:

George Bailey grew up in a small town, forever dreaming of seeing the world and doing big things. But George didn't get to live the life he wanted to live. Because of family obligations and health problems, he was stuck in his god-forsaken hometown while friends and family went away to find adventure. He did good work along the way, but he wasn't doing what he really wanted.

About 30 minutes into the movie, George experiences a crisis where he believes his only option is to end his life. (It sounds extreme here, but it makes sense if you're watching the movie.)

George stands on a bridge over a rushing, frigid river, thinking about jumping. Suddenly, he sees a man drowning in the river beneath him, screaming for help. George immediately jumps into the river and saves the man.

The drowning man is an awkward but lovable angel named Clarence who was sent to earth to help George see that his life is actually worth living. You'll have to watch the rest of the movie to see how it ends, but I'm not afraid to admit that I cry every time I watch it.

Why do people keep watching this movie?

There are so many reasons *not* to watch it. The movie was made in 1946 in black and white and used primitive special effects. It was obviously shot on a movie set, and it had characters that were more caricature than real.

And still, people watch again and again.

It's the subtext that hooks us. And it's this hidden subtext you can turn into a habit.

George is at the end of his rope—and we all know that terrible feeling of lost hope. He's ready to give up completely. For George, dying seems a better option than living.

That's when Clarence introduces the theme that will be repeated throughout the movie: **When you think your life couldn't be worse,**

find someone else who needs help and pour yourself fully into supporting *them*.

When George wanted to end it all, Clarence knew exactly what to do to help him. He forced George to deal with a drowning man. (Do not attempt this at home!)

George had to shift his attention from what was terribly wrong with *his* life to how he could help another person struggling with *theirs*.

Our brains are wired to feel empathy.

Because you feel empathy, you can understand why George risked his life to save Clarence. Empathy will even cause strangers to help strangers like we saw many heroes do during natural disasters in Chapter 21, acting like first responders in crisis.

Your generosity isn't a one-way street.

Just ask George.

When you shift your attention from how terrible and meaningless your life is to supporting that person nearby who needs help, everything changes.

At first, George felt greatly inconvenienced by helping Clarence, and you may have felt that at first when sticking yourself out there for someone else. But his outlook had already begun to expand.

You can't help but change your perspective when you offer someone your sincere support.

The rest of the movie is devoted to showing George how his small acts of service over the years created big changes in people's lives. Without realizing it, they'd changed his life too.

It works in high-stakes situations as well.

A friend of mine, Lt. Colonel Scott Mann Green Beret (Retired), was invited to speak at an elite warrior race. At this event, otherwise sane men and women willingly subjected themselves to two days of intense physical, mental, and emotional challenges with no sleep.

It's *really* challenging.

The typical drop-out rate for this event is over 60%.

Early in the event, Scott offered them one piece of wisdom he learned in the Special Forces: "When you're feeling completely exhausted and ready to quit, turn to the man or woman next to you and ask them, 'How are you doing?' and then take care of them."

Race participants took his words of advice to heart. Every time someone was ready to quit, they'd turn to their neighbor to check in and offer support.

Not one person dropped out of the race.

In fact, the organizers extended the event by several hours, adding more intense challenges trying to get someone to quit. In their great suffering, people kept turning to their neighbors and offering support. No one would give up.

Finally, the organizers had to give up.

Every person went far beyond their individual performance because they'd put their focus on propping up the people around them.

It's a time-tested lesson.

A great spiritual master was once asked by a student who was suffering, "Teacher, I feel so terrible. What can I do to feel better?"

The teacher's immediate reply was (paraphrased): "Find someone else who is suffering more than you are and help them."

Still skeptical? Let science explain it.

Your limbic brain, a.k.a. your mammalian brain, is wired to make connections with other people. This wiring that seeks connection can cause you to want to help someone in need.

This instinct helped primitive humans and other mammals bond to survive together in threatening conditions that solo players would have surely died in.

The limbic brain is where you feel emotions, so it gets a bad rap from some people who say it's too primitive, too emotional. They claim those feelings get in the way of good decision-making.

But it's those emotions that saved George and all of those people in the warrior run.

As an aside, do you know what they call people who believe emotions get in the way of good decisions?

Bad leaders. But I digress...

The need in each of us to have a purpose greater than ourselves is so strong that it can snap you out of the funk you're in.

A drowning Clarence snapped George out of his funk. Elite warriors rely on it to keep going when they're exhausted and losing hope. Spiritual masters have been teaching this as a path to fulfillment for millennia. Even modern brain scientists will tell you it works.

How can you apply this in today's world?

You probably have some audacious goals you plan to achieve.

If they're really audacious, you already know that you're going to face daunting challenges along the way. If it were easy, someone else would have already done it.

You're going to get discouraged.

Things may get so bad that you want to quit. You may fail repeatedly. At the very least, you might fall into a funk as things get difficult.

What will you do when things get really bad?

How about turning to someone nearby and asking them, "How are you doing? How can I help you right now?"

Could you make this your practice for the next 75 days? Or even the next 75 minutes?

If you make this a habit, count on four things:

1) You'll have a greater impact on the things that matter to you.

2) You will feel happier on most days.

3) Your will experience a deeper sense of meaning and purpose for your life.

4) People will start showing up for you when you need help.

But otherwise, nothing really changes.

Who's the first person you're going to offer support to? Why don't you track them down right now?

32

HER PATH TO #1: SHE LOST MORE THAN THE REST

On September 12, 2016, Angelique Kerber won her first US Open Title and earned her first-ever #1 world tennis ranking.

At 28, she was the oldest woman to ever achieve the #1 ranking for the first time.

Ever worry your ship already sailed without you?

Kerber's path to the top reminds us that there is always another ship to catch. That is, if you keep playing.

She shows us that late bloomers aren't just slow or lucky. They've been preparing for years, readying themselves for their opportunities.

The dirty little secret of champions.

There is a secret no one ever mentions about champions like Kerber: The path to the top means losing and failing a lot. More than most.

That's why there are so few late bloomers. Most people think losing is for… losers.

Late bloomers realize they'll either win or they'll learn. Either one is good.

It was a long, long road to the top.

Kerber began her professional career in 2003 at age 15. It took her 13 years of consistent professional play to achieve #1.

Serena Williams was 20 when she received her first #1 ranking. Venus Williams was 21. Chris Evert was 20.

In the body-pounding world of professional tennis, you expect a 28-year-old to be thinking about retirement, not achieving her peak lifetime performance.

It's mindset, not talent, that makes most people miss their ship.

Most 28-year-old tennis players—and many regular people like you and me—would have convinced themselves the missed opportunity was lost forever.

If you rely on standard social norms of time and achievement, it's easy to understand why they give up. For example, "I should have achieved XYZ by age 25 (or 40 or 60). If I didn't, I'm washed up."

Kerber reminds us that we're never done.

Until the last few years, Kerber wasn't even considered a top-tier player. She'd never reached a Grand Slam final before that season.

That year, she played in three Grand Slam finals and won two. Bam!

She made one small tweak.

Early in 2016, she decided to be more assertive. Into that new mindset, she poured the strength built from her years of training and competition.

That little tweak created an expanded window for her well-developed talent to shine through, unrestricted.

Without the years of dedicated training, that little change in attitude would have probably meant nothing. But the years of training plus the mindset tweak launched her leap in performance to the very top.

Her ship hasn't sailed after all.

And neither has yours, unless you decide it has. You've done all of the training. What's the next thing you'll do with it?

Angelique Kerber could have easily told herself that 28 was too old to be #1. And she would have been right.

But she kept showing up. And showing up. And showing up. Until she caught the next ship.

What is your ship?

Every one of us has missed ships we'd hoped to catch. Those misses can be painful. Excruciating. You can convince yourself that your ship has sailed without you.

Or, you can keep showing up. And showing up. And catch the next ship… or the next one…

33

FAILURE IS NOT AN OPTION?
CHAMPIONS KNOW OTHERWISE

Champions fail better.

The secret to winning isn't a secret. It's more like inconvenient wisdom many people forget or deny.

Here it is, simply put: ***Everybody fails, but winners fail better.***

When you stretch yourself to accomplish great things, you're going to stumble and fall—often.

Failure is inevitable. But it's not failing that keeps you from achieving your goals. *How* you fail determines how fast and how well you achieve what you want.

Winners who failed better than their peers.

In 2015, Serena Williams was named the Sports Illustrated Sportsperson of the Year—the best of all world-class athletes. But in 2005, the common wisdom was that her career was fading. What happened?

Despite years of serious injuries and embarrassing losses, Serena persevered and eventually regained her #1 ranking and 13 additional Grand Slam titles.

Every tennis player fails. She failed better.

Abraham Lincoln is consistently ranked as the #1 greatest of all US Presidents.

Yet before he was elected to the Oval Office, he lost two elections for US Senator and one for state legislator. As commander-in-chief during the first years of the Civil War, he suffered historic, devastating failures.

Had Abraham Lincoln not been good at failing, would there have been a Gettysburg Address or an Emancipation Proclamation? Would the United States Constitution have a thirteenth amendment?

Every leader eventually fails. He failed better.

Steve Jobs created the highest-valued company on the planet and products that forever changed the way we live. Even he had some epic failures that would have taken most people out of the game completely.

Every business icon fails. He failed better.

What's your orientation to failure?

The three most common choices are:

1) *Avoid it:* Do you stretch yourself less or avoid risk so you don't have to face failure?

2) *Minimize it:* When you do fail, do you try to hide it or patch it and hope you can return things to how they were before?

3) *Leverage it:* Do you lean into it so you can become stronger, clearer, and wiser for the next round?

Nature: You and I are biologically wired to choose #1 or #2.

Nurture: In most circumstances, society teaches us to choose #1 or #2.

Future: Leaders who shape their own futures train themselves to choose #3.

Shape your future: Train yourself to fail better.

It is unnatural for people to leap into the air without being able to see the ground, but gymnasts train themselves to do it.

It is unnatural for people to run *into* a burning building, but firefighters train themselves to do it.

It is unnatural for people to lean into failure and to leverage it, but you can train yourself to fail better.

To make the huge contributions with your life that you dream of, you must train yourself to fail even better. In what part of your life do you need to remember this right now?

How well can you fail? Your success and satisfaction depends on it.

34

A GIFT IN DISGUISE: THE PAINFUL FAILURE THAT CHANGED ME

In 1996, 30 days after launching my consulting and coaching firm, I nervously walked into my first-ever consulting gig ready to change the world.

I was also eager to prove all of the doubters who said my new venture would fail wrong.

Hopefully, the people you're counting on won't make the mistake I made.

I felt simultaneously confident, intimidated, and incredulous that I'd just landed such a huge job so quickly.

I'd been hired by the EVP of Marketing for a big name, fast-growing technology firm to help turn rising customer complaints around. Let's call him "Terry." Prior to this role, Terry led marketing for a Fortune 25 company with primo brand recognition.

I flew to HQ to kick things off, but he had another agenda.

My first day there, we had a working lunch with Terry and his team. Out of nowhere, he shared a "breakthrough idea" he had for how to interact with customers that he believed would revolutionize the industry.

He asked us to "think about it."

But he couldn't wait. At 3 p.m., he called together the same group and said he'd decided to share his idea with the sales, marketing, and customer management leadership teams who were scheduled to meet for another purpose at 4 p.m. that same day.

I wish I could get a "do-over."

At about 3:45, Terry asked each person one at a time, "What do you think of my idea?" He was giving each of us the power to "pull the cord" and stop him from making the announcement at 4 p.m.

I was sitting at his right, and he started with the person to his left. There were eight of us in the room. One at a time, each person weighed in.

"I like it."

"Yes, let's do it."

"Go for it."

"I'm in."

Every person signed off on this idea that I was almost *certain* was going to bomb.

Then, it was my turn.

Next to me sat a marketing icon, also the first senior executive to ever hire my new consulting firm. I not only knew he was about to fail—I also knew why. So, why had everyone else signed on to his terrible idea so easily?

"And how about you, David?" I lived 20 lifetimes in the two seconds it took for me to respond.

"Yep, I like it."

He slapped his hand enthusiastically on the table and exclaimed, "Great, let's go do this!" as he rose and headed for the big meeting in the next building.

I had told him what he wanted to hear instead of being honest.

About 30 minutes later, I stood in the back of the company lunchroom and watched the meeting break into chaos with my beloved client (who

134

trusted me and hired me to help him win) get chewed up in the front of the room. I winced as I watched it unfold.

That night in my hotel room, I reflected painfully on the day.

What had happened? I failed so badly at doing my job, it was excruciating. *I had failed to speak truth to power.* I'd failed to do what he'd paid me for.

I pledged in that moment that I would *never* let that happen again with one of my clients—no matter how painful it was for them or for me.

Fortunately, I was able to recover from my gaffe.

Our work eventually did turn things around in spite of our bumpy start. But had I done my job, it never would have happened.

What about you?

How ready and willing are you to speak truth to power? How easy do you make it for people to do the same for you?

If you want to have an impact in your world, this is a must-have skill.

Pain is a great teacher.

I've kept my promise to myself, and I've delivered the bad news to many clients since then.

Last week, I had a very honest conversation with a client. He'd asked me my opinion about some choices he'd made. I told him what I believed he needed to hear, not what he wanted to hear. A few days later, I got a text from him thanking me for telling him what he needed to hear, even though he hated hearing it.

To myself, I thanked Terry and the opportunity to fail that he'd given me.

35

5 REASONS YOUR NEW JOB OFFER WILL TAKE WAY LONGER THAN YOU THINK IT SHOULD

Sometimes, failure shows up as endless delays.

Senior executives are used to getting what they want. Not that it's a bad thing. But it's not unusual for you to get frustrated when you interview and negotiate for a role in a new firm, *right?* That's often when my phone rings.

I'm not a recruiter; however, I often serve in a trusted adviser role for senior executives. While each executive calls for different reasons, they almost universally complain about how much longer the process is taking than they were told it would. They often conclude that the hiring company is completely inept or the people who work there are liars. They're convinced they're not going to get this job.

Even if you're not interviewing for a new role today, tuck this away because you'll likely need this reminder in the future. What looks like a failed job search is often just a poorly understood or poorly explained process.

Things that are certain: death, taxes, and delayed interview schedules.
Interviews for senior executive roles will *always* take longer than predicted, and it's not because anyone is stupid or dishonest. Here are five hidden speed bumps that slow down the senior executive interview process.

Special note: If you're on the hiring side, perhaps this will help you forge a better bond with your potential new team member who's suffering through your arcane interview process. The delays that make sense to you are driving your candidates crazy, so make sure they understand what is happening.

Five Reasons Why Your Interview Process Is Going More Slowly than You Want It To:

1. **We all lie to ourselves:** You probably lied to yourself today. If you're like most people, by 9 or 10 a.m., the day you told yourself you'd be having and the day you're actually having are two completely different things.

   Because you don't work in a vacuum, other people's needs, agendas, and processes intrude on your idealized day and force you to change your plans. If your day has veered from its plan by 9 a.m., imagine how that can happen with an interview process involving a team of senior executives, multiple departments, and hectic travel schedules.

   Oh yeah—these people are also running a large company in a competitive, unpredictable market. **Be honest with yourself, and expect a change in plans.**

2. **Caution means slow:** The role you're being hired for is extremely important, and the cost of making a bad hire is enormous.

   If the person you were replacing was terrible, people don't want to repeat the mistake. If the person you're replacing was amazing, they're nervous about filling big shoes. Either way, it makes the hiring decision feel extremely weighty, which triggers caution.

   Is that such a bad thing? **The longer things take, the more opportunities both parties have to see the other's true colors.**

3. **Tailoring takes time:** At this senior level, no two candidates offer the same talent. The hiring firm will probably tailor this job to whomever they hire. For example, my client originally interviewed for a CIO role with a large Asian conglomerate. After the hiring firm learned of his operations experience, they paused the process to consider re-scoping the job into a CIO/COO role. **A job that is tailored to you is a good thing, but tailoring takes extra time.**

4. **Big hires trigger strategy conversations:** Executives are always running fast and rarely get as much time as they want to reassess strategy. Even well-run firms find that discussions with bright, creative candidates—plus the accompanying prep and post-mortem discussions—spark new thinking.

   Behind the scenes, hiring a new executive causes leaders to ask themselves if they need to make any strategic shifts. As long as it's productive, that's also a good thing. **The interview process becomes a catalyst for updated thinking among key leaders.**

5. **This is not college recruiting:** While the hiring company may have a well-run process and team in place to recruit and train 500 new college hires each year, they haven't hired for your role in several years. **There is no prescribed process in place**, and given the above factors, even if there were, thoughtful leaders would not let it force them to make a big decision in haste.

You've witnessed the high cost of bad hiring decisions to both the employer and the employee. While slower doesn't mean better, rushing the decisions is almost never a winning tactic.

Don't waste your energy by making the delays more than they are.

If the job is a fit, things will likely come together. Once you understand the game, you can let the timing work to your advantage. In the meantime, impatiently grinding your gears isn't helping. Go enjoy the sunset and chill for awhile.

36

HE DIDN'T KNOW ANY BETTER, AND HE PAID FOR IT

Cooper (a.k.a. Coop) was a strapping 16-year-old kid who just didn't know any better.

His *one dream* was to play college basketball. Okay, in full disclosure, he also seemed to dream about Mexican food pretty often.

He knew the first step to his big dream was to play high school basketball. And he wanted to be ready.

He logged thousands of hours of practice and play through eighth grade. Thousands.

He got his chance in ninth grade.

Finally, after years of preparation, he tried out for the freshman basketball team.

But the coach didn't see it. Coop was cut from the team in the last round of tryouts.

Bam! Just like that. One person can dash your dream. We've all been there before.

Many kids who got cut found a new dream.

They took themselves out. Or they followed the advice of well-meaning people who didn't want them to waste their time or be disappointed chasing a pipe dream.

Cooper didn't know any better, so he kept playing.

In fact, he worked harder than he ever had—pushing his strength and conditioning, ball handling, and shooting at the hoop by his garage.

He missed his entire ninth-grade basketball season. He wore no uniform, but he probably worked harder than he would have had he made the team.

Does it have a happy ending?

As a sophomore, Cooper had his chance for redemption. Could he squeak by this time?

He tried out again. His competition would be the kids who'd been playing all year.

He needed a winning strategy.

A smart strategy for Coop, who hadn't seen any action as a freshman, was to try to knock off the weakest players and sneak on to the sophomore team.

Apparently, he's not very strategic. He made the varsity—as a starter! True story.

Coop was riding high and living his dream. But there's more.

He was playing full-out.

In game five of the season, Coop's team was trouncing its opponent by 40 points. The smart kids probably held back a bit and saved it for the next game.

Cooper didn't know any better.

He kept playing hard. During a fast break by the opposing team, he sprinted down the floor to catch a player just as he released the ball on a layup. Coop looked like a 200-pound bird in flight.

He stretched so far to successfully block the shot that he landed off balance—on the other kid's foot.

Pop! In an instant, he'd blown out two ligaments (ACL and MCL) in his right knee. And he'd blown his sophomore year.

Now, it's really time to quit.

Any realistic person would know that it was time to quit now. But Cooper just doesn't seem to know any better.

Before they could even schedule his reconstructive surgery, he was already back at it, on one leg, practicing his shot. Going to the weight bench to build his upper body. Practicing his ball-handling drills.

He completed his recovery much faster than expected according to both his surgeon and physical therapist. *Are you really surprised?*

He *really* doesn't know any better.

I forgot to mention that at age 7, Cooper broke his right arm. Being a right-handed shooter, he stopped playing basketball for six weeks during recovery.

Come on! You don't really believe that, do you?

Actually, he didn't know any better, so he taught himself to shoot with his *left* hand. It remains his shooting hand today.

The 30-foot shots he now drains from all over the court are with his *non-dominant* hand. He ain't bad with his right hand, either.

Cooper teaches us that the path isn't always what we imagined, but most dead ends are self-imposed. Simply not knowing any better is the underdog's best friend.

My money is on Cooper to play college basketball. If I were a college coach, I'd be looking at him already.

But what about you?

Are you smart enough to believe it when caring and concerned people who don't want you to be disappointed tell you to pick a new dream?

Or are you foolish like Cooper? I hope you just don't know any better either.

◉ SECTION VI:
YOUR INVISIBLE ADVANTAGE: PREPARATION & RITUALS

Any farmer or gardener knows that planting seeds is important, but that alone doesn't guarantee a plentiful harvest. **It's what they do before and after the planting that has the greatest influence on whether that seed thrives or lies dormant.**

The same is true for you and your genius. It's the preparation you bring day after day, decade after decade, that will determine how much your meaning, mission, and contribution grow.

Have you ever been up close to an elite performer? An athlete or a musician or an actor?

What we see of them in the media represents less than 10% of the life they live. When they step on the platform to receive a medal, or when they take bow after bow on the stage while the fans cheer, they make it look easy and fun. They're smiling. They're standing tall.

A commentator might say, "Well, Bo's big brother also played professional football, which set him up for this success." Or, "Bonnie's dad was a Broadway star, so it's in her blood to be a performer."

go to www.davidmartinco.com/ftg-videos

Those comments are doing everyone with a dream an enormous disservice in that moment. And they're showing their own ignorance. Genetics and family of origin are only small determinants of success.

You can dream, you can feel alive with enthusiasm, you can identify with the underdog on a mission. **But in the end, what brings it all to life is the part that no one ever sees: practice.**

Until you practice like you couldn't live without it, your genius will never be fully set free.

This section brings us full circle to the first section of the book. The Mastery Mindset is critical to cultivating the very best of you. And the essential tool of the Mastery Mindset is practice.

When you are practicing well, you do the small things that matter, usually when no one else is watching, often long before and after the others have started and finished. You make it a ritual that no longer requires a conscious choice. It's become a habit you can't live without.

Practice is usually not fun. It can be painful. Tedious. Repetitive. Frustrating. Humiliating. Exhausting. That's why Chapter 1 reminds us that the path to mastery is never crowded.

Yet, **nothing outranks practice as a determinant of your capacity to free your genius.**

When you grow your success, people may wonder how you got there, because you do most of your practice alone, out of the public eye. They didn't see you practicing tirelessly even on the days when you didn't want to.

These final chapters are the exclamation point of this book. I hope they'll inspire you to look at the choices you make that help you live your most full and satisfying life. Practicing well leads you to your promised land like nothing else.

37

FOIBLES AND FLAWS DO NOT MAKE YOU A FAILURE

Foibles and flaws do not make you a failure. But lack of preparation can make you fail.

I love reading biographies of great people—warriors, titans, artists, athletes, crusaders for a cause.

There's a theme that runs through them.

Not only did those people have historic impact but they're also full of foibles and flaws.

Sometimes, it's shocking what poor judgment or bad behaviors such brilliant people could exhibit. That is, at least when they were out of the public view.

And still, they changed the world.

This matters to you and me.

It's easy to tell yourself that _____ (fill in the blank with your favorite icon or respected friend) could change the world—but that you can't.

After all, this person had all of those superhuman qualities of intelligence, speed, creativity, courage, and so on. They've had buildings or cities or shoes named after them.

But you? You can't even get your kids to say hi when you walk in the door.

You see the double standard, right?

You judge those epic figures by their public images. That's usually a scrubbed, managed presentation of who they are. Rarely does someone reveal their whole self on Instagram!

By contrast, you have much more information available about yourself. It's not limited to your public image. You also get to listen to your inner thoughts, which can get pretty nasty toward yourself or others.

You watch yourself when you're being unreasonable or overly reactive. Plus, you've had a front-row seat to every failure of your entire life.

Of course, you'll lose in any comparison between the whole of you and the press-kit version of them.

Think I'm making this up?

Go read a biography of any person you revere. If it is well-researched and reported honestly, you'll find a person who did brilliant things and who screwed up plenty.*

But there is something that matters…

There's no silver-bullet list of successful qualities, but there are some common threads that run through the history-makers we respect.

One, in particular, is their habits.

Their daily habits. Their habits of thinking. Their habits of connecting with others. Their habits of preparation. The habits that mattered to them.

They didn't share the exact same habits. But they relied on specific habits, thoughtfully chosen to shape them.

That's also true for every high performer I've ever worked with. The habits you choose to repeat deliberately are a key differentiator.

Think of anything great you do today.

You didn't just luck into it. You used one or more habits to build that talent.

---

* For a list of my favorite biographies, go to:
www.davidmartinco.com/booksthatcultivategenius

What do you do over and over?

What you do repeatedly is a habit, even if you never consciously chose to do it. It's defining the person you are. It's shaping the person you're becoming.

Almost 2,500 years ago, Aristotle said, "We are what we repeatedly do. Excellence, then, is not an act but a habit."

This isn't a new idea. It's just one that few people leverage.

If you want someone to write a book about you someday, it's time to set up your life so you can repeat the smart, small actions that make you better over and over and over.

Take an inventory of your habits now. What are you doing repeatedly now that is shaping the person you are becoming?

You can answer this for yourself better than anyone.

Who is the amazing history-maker you're determined to become? What are the small number of things you'll need to do repeatedly to cultivate those qualities in yourself even when no one else is doing them?

Answer this question well, and you could change your future. The chapters in this section will share ideas for habits you can employ.

Once you choose yours: Lather. Rinse. Repeat. Repeat. Repeat...

38

HABITS THAT MAKE YOU WISE & POWERFUL BEYOND YOUR YEARS

Let's talk about time travel. Impossible, right?

But what would you do if it were possible? How powerful could you be?

Actually, there's a way to travel forward in time, and you can do it as often as you want.

Here's the alternative...

I attended a college reunion recently. One afternoon, I walked across the quad following a couple of alumni in their 70s.

As they walked, two young college students ran right in front of them, chasing each other and laughing. It stopped both alums in their tracks.

As they stood there smiling, one said to the other with a twinkle in his eye, *"Man, I wish I knew then what I know now. College would have been a LOT more fun!"*

We've all said that, haven't we?

Wouldn't it be great to go back in time with the knowledge of today and relive an old experience?

Those two alumni almost cracked the code. Here's what they missed.

While traveling backward from today to the past may not be possible, what if you were able to travel backward from the future to today? Wouldn't the effect be the same? You could apply that knowledge of the future now.

How is it possible to live today with the knowledge you will have in the future? From the future you—20 or 30 years in advance.

Imagine what it would be like to walk into any situation today with the knowledge of your older and wiser self. What would be different in your daily life? How could you contribute differently?

If jumping forward 20 or 30 years seems extreme, what about one year?

How much more wise are you today than you were just one year ago? Wouldn't you make some better choices with your recently earned wisdom?

You can actually do this.

In fact, you know people who are already doing it. When you're around them, you probably say, "Wow, they're so wise for their years!"

How did they become so wise? They are great students of the world and life. They don't need graduate degrees or a wall full of framed diplomas.

They have no doubt done the following:

- They probably study with extraordinary teachers.

- They do plenty of extra study and practice on their own.

- They are great observers who pay deep attention to the world outside them and within them.

- They read **great books.**

Reading great books is an incredible way to travel in time.

When you read a great book, you gather knowledge that will make you much wiser today.

If you prefer, you can wait 5 or 10 or 20 years until you've had the same experiences the author already had and learn it on your own.

Or you can read a great book and gain that knowledge now.

What is a great book? A great book is written by an author who has lived and worked in their field for decades.

They've researched it.

They've lived it.

They've taught people about it.

Especially when they teach other people, it forces them to find the clearest words to make their ideas resonate with you.

Then, they write about it.

They thoughtfully draw from all of their experiences and distill their lifetime of insights into pearls of wisdom that they offer us in a few hundred pages. Especially when they teach with stories, you will absorb and retain their ideas for years.

That is a gift!

When you read their books, you leap into the future today.

You've gained knowledge that would've taken you years more of living to acquire. You create the future version of yourself now.

Instead of wistfully saying, "I wish I knew then what I know now," you can say, "I'm glad I know today what I wouldn't have known for years."

That's how you become the wiser version of yourself now. You travel in time.

Will you to commit to reading great books today?

If you could only do one thing to make yourself a better leader, I suggest you start reading* immediately. Even if you have only five minutes a day, it will pay you great dividends forever.

Need some suggestions? You can download my latest book list (I update it periodically) here: www.davidmartinco.com/booksthatcultivategenius.

---

* I "read" many books on audible.com at 2X and 3X speed. I can listen while I'm traveling or driving. Perhaps listening to books will be easier for you than reading them.

39

USE THE APPLE WATCH'S HIDDEN STRATEGIES TO BUILD POWER RITUALS

The Fitbit app was the #1 downloaded app after Christmas 2015. Since then, the Apple Watch and other smart watches have gone mainstream.

It's no wonder everyone wants a smart watch. People are producing amazing results in weight loss and health simply because they pay attention to a little band wrapped around their wrist.

It's not the gadgetry. It's the strategy.

The Apple Watch is easy and effective, but the magic isn't just in the technology. Smart watch technology works because the designers cleverly use a mash-up of three proven high-performance strategies to help you change critical, stubborn behaviors so that you're finally able to achieve those elusive results.

But wait! These strategies don't just work for tangible results like weight loss.

Leaders with no gadgets on their wrists have applied these same strategies to achieve intangible results like:

- greater power/influence and more compelling leadership skills
- accelerated business results and career breakthroughs.

What are the high-performance strategies smart watches leverage so well?

1. **From unclear to measurable:** Smart watches take the old adage, "People produce what you measure" to a new extreme. You can now easily measure and monitor Key Performance Drivers (KPDs) that greatly affect your health, like step count, heart rate, standing time, and water intake.

   Apply this to your leadership behaviors. What are the little behavioral shifts in KPDs that must occur for you to achieve the elusive, intangible leadership goals you seek? How can you make your KPDs measurable?

2. **From private to public:** Our health or our weight is no longer a taboo subject we only discuss with a close friend, doctor, or trainer. Smart watches make measuring healthy activities part of the public conversation by displaying it on our wrists and letting us share progress with friends. We share how many steps we took today (a KPD of health) like we used to talk about what we watched on TV last night.

   Apply this to your leadership. How can you make your intangible goals public so that others can support you—and hold you accountable?

3. **From work to a game:** Simply turning an activity into a game, especially if it's a mundane or challenging activity (e.g., exercising or drinking water), elicits higher participation from people. Gamification has become a multi-billion dollar industry because it works. The easiest way to turn your work into a game is to add the component of challenge to it so that it's not quite as easy to succeed, e.g., go for a streak of doing some minimum KPD every day or put an end date/deadline to when you'll achieve the new

goal. Adding any parameter or restriction that adds some challenge to your achievement moves it toward being a game.

Apply this to your leadership practices. What parameters or restrictions can you add to your activities so it feels like more of a challenge to overcome than just an obligation?

Ready to achieve a new personal or team best?

You can apply these strategies for a variety of results. For example, they'll help you:

- close sales and build revenues faster
- implement big, strategic change initiatives more smoothly
- repair broken customer relationships
- meet project deadlines more quickly
- have fewer and more productive meetings

What are the big results you want to deliver this year?

Whether they're tangible or intangible, leverage these three strategies to get there faster and easier, just like the Apple Watch does for weight loss and better health.

40

THE HIGH-PERFORMANCE HACK YOU CAN STEAL FROM MY GRANDPA

My Grandpa Nye was 67 years older than I was, and he came from a different world, pre-electricity, pre-autos, pre-indoor plumbing.

He earned no diploma because he dropped out of school in eighth grade to help on his family farm. But he cultivated a deep life wisdom from years of struggle. As a result, he was always teaching.

Old-world thinking. New-world application.

Years later, many Fortune 50 executives have told me how the lessons I learned from Grandpa Nye have proven valuable to them.

Grandpa Nye lived 200 feet north of our farmhouse, and he worked on the farm with my dad, so I was with him a lot. He was my Yoda in overalls.

He was a high performer ahead of his time.

If the term "high performer" existed in his day, Grandpa Nye would have earned that label. Never hurried, he rocked from side to side as he walked because of advanced arthritis in both knees and hips.

He and my dad farmed a large acreage across three separate farms using modest machinery compared to the monster farm implements of today. But every year, they got it done and did it well.

Grandpa's High-Performance Hack

Read carefully to see if you can catch the hack.

Every day on the farm that he worked on the farm, Grandpa Nye wore blue-and-white-striped OshKosh B'Gosh overalls over a long-sleeved green shirt.

If he went to town to socialize, he'd change into his green work pants that matched his green shirt with a nicer pair of work boots.

On Sundays, he wore a suit and tie to church, then he'd come home and change into the green/green combo for the rest of the day.

There it is! Did you catch his high-performance hack?

His hack was this: *He knew when he wasn't working.* The different clothes he wore in each situation were his reminder to think and act differently. Years later, Mr. Rogers employed a similar strategy.

High performers know that regularly stepping away from their work is a highly productive move.

You know this too. Even when you've stopped working, your brain keeps subconsciously chipping away at unsolved problems. Your body and brain get to recharge. You gain a perspective that you can't get with your nose pressed against the glass and your brain spinning wildly.

Grandpa Nye's hack amplified both high performance and happiness. He laughed often.

Old-School Common Sense for a New Day

Grandpa would laugh hard if he knew I was sharing his rituals as a big idea. Stepping away from his work was just common sense for him. But because of technology that lets us take our work to bed and a world economy that never sleeps, it's hard to know when to not work. Maybe you need some old-school wisdom for today.

Practice the Hack—Now!

With the end of the work day, end of the work week, or an upcoming vacation or break, you're probably going to take some time off soon. Can you seize this opportunity to really not work? You know it's worth it.

If it helps, hide your laptop. Go extreme and remove the email app from your smartphone for 24 hours. Remove the temptation to bypass this "not working" hack. Change your wardrobe if that helps.

Trade your constant connection to work for some highly unproductive but enjoyable not-working activities. You'll increase your performance, and maybe you'll even laugh like an old farmer.

What do you most need a break from? Start there.

41

WILL YOU BE PREPARED WHEN YOUR LIFE-CHANGING OPPORTUNITY ARRIVES?

In the 2017 NCAA Women's Final Four, Morgan William from Mississippi State caught the basketball at mid-court with 3.9 seconds left in a tied game. Her window of opportunity to change history opened and closed in less time than it took you to read this paragraph.

Her story is one that can inspire and instruct every one of us who wants to make our dent in the universe.

She did not throw away her shot.

Morgan caught the ball near half court, faked left, then ran seven steps on three dribbles to her right. She pulled up and took a 15-foot jump shot over a towering giant's hand with 1.2 seconds on the clock.

The ball floated to the hoop and swished in as the buzzer went off.

David had defeated Goliath.

On that shot, Mississippi State beat UConn (NCAA Women's Basketball Champions in 2013, 2014, 2015, and 2016) by two points in overtime.

Importantly, in the NCAA tournament the year before, UConn beat Mississippi State by 60 points, 98-38. Not this year! Morgan's winning shot propelled Mississippi State to its first-ever NCAA Final game.

In the 2.7 seconds she had the ball, Morgan William ended Goliath's reign and settled a score.

She was ready for her tap on the shoulder. Will you be?

Morgan William had 3.9 seconds to do her work. She caught and shot the ball in the time it takes you to sing the first line of the "Happy Birthday" song.

But if you focus on those 3.9 seconds, you've missed the point. Morgan prepared *for years and years so she was ready to seize those 3.9 seconds.* She'd practiced countless hours with her father long before she went to college.

She referenced that work with her father.

"All the hours he made me fine-tune the little parts of my game—the footwork and the conditioning."

When her father died three years earlier, she wanted to quit playing the game. Who could blame her? But she returned to the gym, heartbroken yet dedicated to continue the work they started together. That's why she was ready in that game. She had done the work in advance.

Your window will swing open too.

Just like Morgan William, you're going to get tapped on the shoulder to contribute in a bigger way. At least a few times this year, absolutely. It will probably be unexpected.

You may have more than 3.9 seconds to act, but the window will close. If you wait until then to prepare, your opportunity will probably pass you by.

Are you preparing for your tap on the shoulder?

What are the little parts of your life that you're fine-tuning to make sure you're ready?

Here are four reasons most people drop out of preparation:

1. **Time:** You definitely don't have time for it. (You make time for it.)
2. **Boredom:** You'll sometimes get bored with it. Or discouraged.

3. **Solitude:** You'll probably be alone when you're preparing.

4. **Doubt:** You'll question whether it's worth it when there's no obvious benefit.

That's why there is only one Morgan William. She didn't let these obstacles stop her. She shaped herself into the one who was ready.

There's also only one of you.

Morgan's dad told her, "The ball is going to keep bouncing, whether it's in your hands or someone else's."

In the same vein, someone is going to be ready to make their dent in the universe when the window of opportunity opens. Why shouldn't it be your hands doing the denting?

Here it comes, ready or not!

42

WHAT'S THE SECRET OF YOUR HIGH PERFORMANCE?

A former client of mine is an award-winning writer—and a delightful being. She's also good at surprises.

She makes reading easy even though her topics are complex.

As you read her words, you feel like you're having a casual conversation with a friend. Meanwhile, you're absorbing complicated information.

I wanted to write like she did.

Through our work, we became friends, so when I started writing 10 years ago, I called to ask for advice.

The seeker and the sage.

We chatted for a while before I worked up the nerve to tell her about my own desire to write and then ask her, "Is there a technique you'd suggest I adopt? A teacher you'd recommend I study with? A course to take? A book I should read?"

She was silent as she considered my questions.

As she began to speak, I sat poised at my laptop, ready to type as fast as the genius spilled out of her. She said, "Well, I've tried many different writing techniques over the years. And I've had some great teachers. There are definitely some writing books worth reading.

But in the end, what I think makes me the best writer I can be is… **a deadline.**"

I stopped typing. That was not what I was expecting. I was a bit disappointed.

It's taken me years to appreciate the profundity of her comment.

The deadline is the excuse.

Yes, we could all get better at what we do. But what if we started by claiming the talent we already have that we aren't leveraging consistently?

Don't you do things to yourself that prevent you from playing at your best?

A deadline gets you to focus, to quiet the noise, to eliminate or ignore distractions so you can play at full strength.

The strength was always there. The deadline is the excuse to bring it.

But what if you didn't need the deadline?

Deadlines are a valuable tool. But there's another way to bring all of your talent to bear—it's totally within our control.

You can skillfully manage your mind and your habits instead of letting the noise manage you. With fewer self-imposed obstacles detaining you, the deadlines become less important.

What's your mind noise that holds you back?

What limits your talent or slows you down? Are you self-critical? Do you waste energy comparing yourself to others? Are you stuck in overwhelm? Are you complaining about others or about circumstances? Or are you just distracted?

How do you play at full power?

You've certainly had streaks when you were on fire and unstoppable. Other than the external drivers like deadlines and screaming clients, how do you manage yourself to play your best game?

How are you making those power moves your new, learned habits? Committing to turn them into habits could be your boldest career move yet. And if it helps you turn down the noise, there's always a deadline.

43

PREPARING PEOPLE TO EMBRACE YOUR BOLD IDEAS

If you're on a mission to lead a revolution, you must be masterful at enrolling supporters for your bold ideas.

Your idea is too big to deliver alone. You need advocates, and you can build a strategy and plan to cultivate their support for your great vision.

There's always initial resistance, even to the most brilliant ideas.

You may have to start with easing people's pushback before you worry about gaining their support, especially if your vision is very different from the current circumstances. There are more of them than there are of you, so even just softening their resistance toward neutrality is a huge shift toward succeeding.

The next step is to move these people from no longer resisting to actively supporting. If they feel you're trying to move them too fast, the resistance will resurface. Go slow to go fast.

It's obvious to you why your idea is brilliant.

But it takes wisdom, patience, and finesse to bring new supporters along.

If you don't have a big idea to move forward now, tie a little string around your finger for the next time you have a breakthrough idea that's too big to deliver by yourself. You can re-read this chapter as you begin your mission.

Never take it personally: Breakthrough ideas usually begin as controversial ideas.

Here are seven obvious but important factors you must address if you want to lead this mission and not have your idea become the latest flavor of the month.

Please, please, please use these! These seven steps have helped leaders drive initiatives that have helped tens of millions of people and had multi-billion-dollar business impacts.

Seven Factors That Determine the Success of Your Mission

☐ **#1: People must know they are free to say no:** What?!!! That's crazy, isn't it? You want people to say *yes*, not no.

Actually, this may be the most important factor of all. You don't want people to say yes because they feel trapped. A yes under pressure eventually becomes a no somehow.

If it's a forced yes, they'll find a way to sabotage it later, even if it's unconscious. People are creative, and they'll find a way to stop you if they don't feel they can freely commit or decline.

But a yes of their choosing is priceless. To choose yes emphatically, they need to know that a no is a legitimate option. Put yourself in their shoes if you are still skeptical. How do you like it when your yes is expected? And how strong is your support when it is forced?

☐ **#2: Demonstrate your shared concerns:** They must believe you're truly committed to their well-being and success as much as you are to your own. If they believe you're all about you, they will opt out or stay at arm's length. Demonstrate authentically how some of your concerns overlap. And make sure they understand that their concerns matter deeply to you. If they feel theirs take a back seat to yours, resistance will rise. Guaranteed.

Notice that Factors #1 & #2 have nothing to do with your idea. First, you have to convince your potential supporters' fear-based reptile brains that they are safe. These first two factors address their emotional engagement. Even in businesses that are rooted in analytics, emotions are what cause people to act (or not act). Facts just make them think. You've got to engage them emotionally, and they must feel safe, which is far more emotional than logical.

☐ **#3: Know their inner dialogue:** This is Sales/Influencing 101: Know your customer. Can you describe their hopes, dreams, fears, and struggles in their words? Use *their* words, not your translation of their words. When you describe it, you want them to feel like you've been living in their heads. How do you develop this knowledge? Question 1 is to ask them is "What keeps you up at night?" or "What makes you mad?" Question 2 could be "How could things be better? What does a perfect world look like to you?" Then, build from there. If you're really interested and earn their trust, they'll tell you exactly what you need to do to engage them in your idea.

☐ **#4: Make the idea matter to them:** Connect your idea to what they told you matters to them. Your goal is to ensure that they clearly understand how your idea will make their fears and struggles go away and their hopes and dreams grow. Make sure your idea feels personal to them. The more specific to one person you can be, the more compelling your ideas will be—even if you're speaking to a large group. Generalities are bland and unappealing. Specifics are easier to connect to.

☐ **#5: Tell stories thoughtfully:** You could tell a story about the past, present, and future that they can see themselves in. Your story about the past and present must ring true to their experiences. (Meet them where they are.) Your story about the future shows how your new idea addresses their hopes, dreams, fears, and anxieties. (Show them that what they want is possible and that their fears are being addressed.) Or, since people often connect to other people who share common pain points, you could tell stories about how terrible the struggle has been for them or for your clients.

☐ **#6: Make it easy for them to say yes and to take action:** Make sure there is no confusion in their minds that could make it hard for them to decide. When people are confused in new territory, they stop moving. Make the path forward simple and clear so they don't have to pause and think about what to do next. It may not be clear what to do next week or next month, but they know what to do now. You might only be able to name their next one or two steps. That's enough for today. As they take small steps, you repeatedly make it easier to say yes to this new path than to retreat to the old one, even when things are stressful. The further along the path they've traveled, the more likely they'll be to keep moving forward rather than retreat to their old ways. Make the small steps clear until they're able to direct themselves.

☐ **#7: Find the influencers on the fringe**: Rarely will you get broad support immediately, especially if your idea is controversial or threatening to the status quo. Find the thought leaders and influencers on the fringes who others listen to. They may not be the obvious power brokers, but people trust and listen to them. And if these people resist your ideas, do not dismiss them, even if they're difficult or rude. They actually see things that are lost in your blind spots. Ignoring them will not only cause them to become more resistant; you'll also be ignoring their wisdom that is pointing out legitimate derailers you've overlooked that must be addressed to succeed.

Complete Steps 1 to 6 with the key influencers first. Once they're on board, invite them to help build the enrollment plans for more people.

Please share this checklist with your fellow revolutionaries.

Go make your dent in the universe.

44

THEY GAVE HER THE DREAM, BUT SHE RAN WITH IT

In the 2016 summer games, Gwen Jorgensen won her first Olympic Gold medal in the women's triathlon. In 2009, she was a 23-year-old tax accountant for a Big Four accounting firm. Her Olympic journey began with an unexpected phone call at work.

It's a story of hope for anyone with a dream.

As the story goes, the US Olympic committee was frustrated the US hadn't had more success in the triathlon and went searching for candidates to recruit into their program.

The ideal candidates were runners and swimmers. Jorgensen had been a swimmer and runner at the University of Wisconsin, so her profile was a perfect match.

The Olympics was not in her career plan.

She got a call. Caller ID: US Olympic Headquarters, Colorado Springs, Colorado.

Can you imagine being a first-year accountant at a Big Four firm, immersed in the non-glamorous world of tax accounting and getting that phone call?

Surely this is a prank call, right?

She "got discovered."

The age of the internet and social media has helped to create a fantasy for some people. They believe they're going to be discovered and are waiting for the call to hoist them to the fame and fortune they deserve.

Everyone's heard the story of the one who got discovered.

Getting discovered is a ticket to easy street. Goodbye problems! Hello, Lamborghini!

It's the barista who served a macchiato to a movie mogul and suddenly got cast in a movie opposite Ryan Gosling. It's the window cleaner who posted a grainy Facebook video singing a song he wrote who gets offered a multi-million dollar recording contract.

Haven't we all had that fantasy at some point for ourselves?

What Gwen Jorgensen did *after* she got picked defines how the victorious play this game.

The fantasy is that, if you get the call, you've made it.

She knew the call was just an invitation: You're invited to work your ass off for the next decade and maybe get recognized for it.

It's what she did *after* getting discovered that defined her success.

Here's the reminder for you and me:

It's the rare person who gets a call like Jorgensen or Justin Bieber did.

For most of us, there is no call. No one picks us out of the crowd.

But don't take yourself out of the game just yet.

Pick yourself, dammit.

In reality, many of the chosen few who did get the call never make it out of the phone booth.

They confused being picked with making it. They had their one big hit, and they waited for the next one to roll in. Nothing. Or things got hard, and they quit.

Once you've picked yourself, follow Jorgensen's lead: **Do the work to prepare to succeed.**

Doing the work includes failing, struggling, and wanting to quit. Remember, <u>there are no traffic jams on the path to mastery</u> in Chapter 1.

After one terrible finish, Jorgensen was so discouraged that she told her coach she wanted to quit. He wisely suggested she take a week off before she made a final decision.

We know how that turned out.

Success is in the work.

You know that the people you admire and aspire to be like didn't wait to get picked.

They've been doing the work of preparation when no one else was watching. When their friends and peers were lounging in front of *The Late Late Show*, they were quietly doing the work. Hour after hour. Year after year.

Then, in some unexpected moment, their hard work prepared them to do something none of their peers (who hadn't been running the miles) were prepared to do.

Suddenly, they're an overnight success. But it didn't happen overnight. It just happened out of sight.

Pick yourself, dammit. And get to work.

CONCLUSION

FREE THE GENIUS.
FREE YOUR GENIUS.

Some people tie a string around their finger to remember something they might forget. Each chapter in this book is like a string to remind you what you forget most often: you are powerful and brilliant many magnitudes beyond what you have yet experienced.

You have all that you need, already. You came fully loaded. That's not your work. Your work is to cultivate, grow, and share your genius with full enthusiasm.

The world needs your genius more than ever. Come back to this book any time you need a reminder of the Genius you are.

I have a personal favor to ask. A book's impact is often determined by the reviews it receives. If you feel so inclined, I would greatly appreciate your online review. You can leave a review wherever the book was the purchased.

Please share your stories with me. How do you free your genius? How has this book impacted you? I'm interested to hear! Contact me at: letsconnect@davidmartinco.com.

 For extra guidance and clarity, check out the free training audios and videos that support this book here:

www.davidmartinco.com/ftg-videos.

ABOUT THE AUTHOR

 **David Martin** is a business coach and consultant for leaders preparing to transform their business— leaders who are ready to go faster or further than their organizations and systems may be prepared for. For over two decades, he's been guiding Fortune 50 executives and entrepreneurs (the visionaries who can see around corners) through the business and people challenges that predictably occur when driving to a new destination.

David and his team begin with the unique understanding that you cannot transform your business without transforming the way you lead. David's pioneering work to help people "free the genius" to accelerate their transformation is a hallmark of his company's work.

David and his team have guided thousands of business leaders across North and South America, Europe, Asia, and Australia in discovering and accessing the untapped genius in themselves and their companies. David also shares essential lessons for leaders through his popular blog posts, training programs, and speeches. His use of stories and metaphors helps people move quickly from frustrated visionary to connected, purposeful leader.

Clients have humorously given David various nicknames for his abilities to "see" what's really happening beneath the surface and for respectfully calling out the hidden obstacles and openings that are slowing or accelerating success. These epithets include *bomb-thrower, secret weapon, star-maker, Yoda, the doctor, and psychic.*

David integrates multiple disciplines beyond mainstream business management, all grounded in the pragmatic schooling he received from his elders, three generations of Midwestern farmers. David and his team are known for delivering just-in-time guidance of the right resources at the right time, helping clients quickly leap to new levels of performance and results. Clients include Abbott Labs, Aetna, Barclaycard, Capital One, Gerdau, GlaxoSmithKline, Passport Labs, P&G, McKesson and Xero.

David Martin can be reached at:
https://www.davidmartinco.com/

Made in the USA
Columbia, SC
01 March 2019